INTERNATIONAL PROJECT FINANCE
IN A NUTSHELL

By

JOHN M. NIEHUSS

Adjunct Professor
University of Michigan Law School

WEST®

A Thomson Reuters business

Mat #41043088

Nutshell Series, In a Nutshell and the Nutshell Logo are trademarks registered in the U.S. Patent and Trademark Office.

© 2010 Thomson Reuters

    610 Opperman Drive
    St. Paul, MN 55123
    1–800–313–9378

Printed in the United States of America

ISBN: 978–0–314–26598–2

DEDICATION

This book is dedicated to, and was inspired by, the memory of my father, Marvin L. Niehuss (1903–2003). He was an educator associated with the University of Michigan for over fifty years as a student, faculty member and administrator serving as Vice President, Dean of Faculties and Executive Vice President. When he retired in 1973, the Regents of the University noted that his "commitment and service to the University have rarely been equaled" and that "few men in the history of the University have come to know it so well or done more to shape its destiny."

PREFACE

This is a book that deals with the legal aspects of a very practical subject: how to raise funds for the construction and operation of major projects using a type of finance known as project finance. This method is commonly used to help fund the investments needed to expand the infrastructure and obtain the energy, minerals and other commodities needed for economic growth in both developed and emerging market economies.

The book introduces the concept of project finance and then focuses on the main legal issues that arise during each phase of a typical international project finance transaction. It is intended as an introduction for law students and lawyers who have had no previous exposure to the field and emphasizes basic concepts while leaving most details to more in-depth books and articles. While the focus is legal in nature, the book may also be of interest to non-lawyers involved in preparing and implementing international projects and public-private partnerships.

The content is based on materials used in a course taught at the University of Michigan Law School and is divided into five main sections as follows:

Part I—Introductory. This section provides an explanation of the concept of project finance and outlines the role of the lawyer in an international project financing transaction.

Part II—Basic Project Preparation. Part II describes the extensive preparatory work that must be done for each project to assess its risks, conduct due diligence, plan for procurement, and create the basic legal structure.

Part III—Project Documents. This part of the book deals with the agreements that establish the relationship with the host government, allocate risk among the project participants, govern the construction and operation of the project, and create the revenue stream that serves as the basis for raising finance for the project.

Part IV—Financing Documents. This section describes the process of arranging finance. It covers the sources of finance and the various agreements that govern the funding, credit support and administration of loans for the project.

Part V—When Problems Arise. The final section deals with the fact that the long term nature of most project financings means that problems inevitably arise and need to be dealt with through renegotiation and restructuring or various dispute settlement mechanisms.

I would like to thank Ned Neaher, a project finance partner at the law firm of White & Case, for his contribution to this work. He read and commented on drafts of the manuscript, spent time answering questions about current practices in the project finance field and provided valuable suggestions which led to changes that substantially improved the final product.

JOHN M. NIEHUSS

May 2010
Washington, D. C.

ABBREVIATIONS

AAOIFI	Accounting and Auditing Board for Islamic Financial Institutions
BIT	Bilateral Investment Treaty
BNDES	O Banco Nacional de Desenvolvimento Economico e Social (Brazilian Development Bank)
CDM	Clean Development Mechanism
CER	Carbon Emission Reduction
ECA	Export Credit Agency
EDFI	European Development Finance Institutions
EPC	Engineering, Procurement and Construction
FIDIC	Federation Internationale des Ingenieurs–Conseils (International Federation of Consulting Engineers)
FM	Force Majeure
IFC	International Finance Corporation
IFI	International Financial Institution

ABBREVIATIONS

ISDA	International Swaps and Derivatives Association, Inc.
JBIC	Japan Bank for International Cooperation
KfW	Kreditanstalt fur Weideraufbau/KfW Bankengruppe
LD	Liquidated Damages
MDB	Multilateral Development Bank
MIGA	Multilateral Investment Guarantee Agency
NAFTA	North American Free Trade Areas
NPC	Negative Pledge Clause
OECD	Organization for Economic Co-operation and Development
OECF	Japanese Overseas Economic Cooperation Fund
OPIC	Overseas Private Investment Corporation
PCG	Partial Credit Guarantee
PRG	Partial Risk Guarantee
PPP	Public–Private Partnership
SPV	Special Project Vehicle

OUTLINE

PART II. PROJECT PREPARATION AND STRUCTURING

PART V. WHEN PROBLEMS ARISE

Chapter 20. Renegotiation and Restructuring

INTERNATIONAL
PROJECT
FINANCE
IN A NUTSHELL

PART I

INTRODUCTORY

CHAPTER 1

OVERVIEW OF INTERNATIONAL PROJECT FINANCE

This chapter provides an overview of an international project finance transaction by introducing the basic concepts and vocabulary that lawyers should be familiar with before beginning to work in the field. It is intended to serve as a foundation for the subsequent discussion of the main legal issues that arise at various stages of the financing.

A. What Is International Project Finance?

Project finance is a special method of raising funds for projects—primarily in the energy, mining and infrastructure sectors. In recent years, it also has been used in connection with public-private partnerships to fund projects where the private sector works with a governmental entity to provide public services traditionally financed by governments. An international project financing is a project with a cross-border dimension involving participants and/or funding from more than one country.

1

1. <u>A Type of Structured Finance</u>. Project finance is part of a larger family of financial techniques known as structured finance. In a structured financing, a revenue generating asset (or group of assets) is segregated in order to serve as the source of debt repayment and shift the repayment obligation away from the entity that created the asset to the revenue stream generated by the asset. This concept is broad enough to include such techniques as mortgage backed securities and collateralized debt obligations as well as project financing. In all of these techniques, the cash flow generated by an asset or pool of assets is used as the basic source of loan repayment rather than the balance sheet of the originator of the transaction. However, in the case of project financing the cash flow is typically generated by a new operating asset created by the project while in most other forms of structured finance the cash flows used to repay debt are generated by pools of existing financial assets like mortgages, loans or various kinds of receivables.

2. <u>Comparison with Traditional Forms of Finance</u>. The basic concept of project finance may also be explained by contrasting it with the methods that government and private sector entities commonly use to fund major projects. When governments undertake projects, they typically rely on allocations from their capital budgets which are funded primarily by tax revenues and domestic and international borrowings. When a private sponsor undertakes a project, it generally funds the project with a combination of its own internal cash resources, borrowing and sometimes new equity. These methods of financing a project are relatively

simple. In both cases, borrowings are based on the overall financial condition and creditworthiness of the government or corporation and its ability to generate cash from all governmental or corporate assets and activities. When the government or corporate sponsors are creditworthy with ample cash reserves and borrowing capacity, these traditional methods are the quickest and least complicated ways to fund major projects.

However, governments and corporate sponsors are often cash constrained and unable or unwilling to raise funds in the markets due to a variety of factors. These factors include poor credit, restrictive covenants in existing loan documents or a desire to avoid excessive concentration of resources and risk in a single project. In such cases, they often turn to project finance to raise the debt needed for the project. This provides an alternative method of funding major projects that relies on the cash flow generated by the project itself and does not depend entirely on the financial capacity or creditworthiness of the government or corporation

To summarize, the unique aspect of any project financing—domestic as well as international—is that it relies on the revenue and assets of a single project to provide equity returns, debt service and security for loans. This contrasts with the methods governments and corporations generally use to raise funds which are often referred to as sovereign borrowing and corporate finance respectively and which establish creditworthiness by relying on the revenues from all of the borrower's projects and activities and on all of its assets as security.

B. Basic Characteristics

There are several inter-related elements that are common to almost all domestic and international project financings and which contribute to their legal complexity. They are:

1. Special Project Vehicle. A new entity is created by the sponsor of the project and is commonly referred to as the Special Project Vehicle (the "SPV") or the Project Entity. The SPV is created to own the project assets, enter into contracts and normally act as the borrower of the debt funds raised for the project. The entity starts its existence as a shell with no assets, no income and no previous operating history and acts as the focal point or hub for the contractual and other activities associated with the project.

2. The Revenue Stream. The revenue stream generated by the new asset created by the project is the primary source of payment of debt service and dividends. It is this fact that may enable the asset and the debt to be off-balance-sheet for the originating sponsor.

3. Non–Recourse or Limited Recourse Financing. Because project financings rely on the revenue and assets of the SPV rather than the overall creditworthiness of the sponsor for the repayment of debt, they are frequently called non-recourse financings. This means that there is no recourse to a sponsor's credit beyond its equity in the SPV. In

reality, it is extremely rare for a project financing to be 100% non-recourse. Rather, sponsors are often asked to provide some credit support which means that there is some limited recourse to the sponsor. This type of transaction is called a limited recourse financing.

4. Risk Identification and Mitigation. Because the assets of a single project are the sole source of revenue, there is an intense focus on the risks that might adversely affect these assets and the revenue stream they generate and on the measures available to avoid or mitigate these risks. This leads to extensive feasibility work and investor and lender due diligence during the preparatory stage of the project.

5. Contract Based Financing. A complex web of inter-related contracts is created between the SPV and other project participants in order to help allocate project risks and to create and protect the revenue stream generated by the project assets. The existence of so many contracts means that project finance is sometimes called contract-based financing.

6. Highly Leveraged Capital Structure. Project financings typically have a large amount of debt relative to equity, and it is common to have 70–80% in debt financing and 20–30% in equity finance. The exact amount of leverage is highly dependent on the basic project economics and the strength of the offtake or user contracts that create the revenue stream for the project.

7. Diversity of Lenders. International project financings generally involve a diverse group of lend-

ers. This is especially true for transactions in emerging markets. Lenders in international financings may include commercial banks, multilateral development banks, export credit agencies, specialized bilateral agencies and purchasers of bond issues.

8. Third Party Credit Support. Lenders are reluctant to rely solely on a project's revenue stream for debt service and require various forms of third party back-up credit support to provide assurance that their debt will be serviced even if the revenue stream never materializes or is diminished or interrupted. Such support includes guarantees, insurance, letters of credit, warranties, surety bonds and derivatives.

9. Project Accounts. Trust, reserve and other accounts are created to collect, segregate and protect the revenues generated by the project assets, establish payment priorities and to channel funds to the lenders for debt service and other priority uses.

10. Security Over Project Assets. To provide an added level of assurance to lenders, security interests are created in favor of the lenders over all project assets, including the concession, the sponsor's shares in the SPV, all project contracts and project accounts.

11. Renegotiation and Restructuring. Given their complexity and generally long duration, many projects need to be renegotiated or restructured at some point to accommodate unforeseen developments in the project or the external environment.

12. Unique Dispute Settlement. Special attention is given to dispute resolution procedures for

international projects due to the presence of participants from different countries subject to different laws and treaties and to the interconnected nature of the contractual relations among the participants.

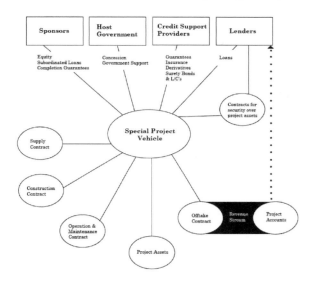

SIMPLIFIED DIAGRAM OF THE CONCEPT
OF PROJECT FINANCE

C. Main Participants

The number of participants with disparate and often conflicting interests is one of the major factors complicating the legal work in any project financing. There are three participants—the host government, the sponsors and the lenders—that are the main decision makers on most key issues and whose decisions determine the overall structure and course of an international project. Other participants are also critical because of their role in providing specific services or functions that are essential to project success. The roles of several of the key participants are described as follows:

1. Host Government. The government of the country in which the project is located is often the key participant in an international project finance transaction as its decisions (or lack of decisions) can determine whether a project is undertaken and whether it is ultimately successful. Its actions determine the overall investment climate, regulatory regime and political stability of the country; and its continuing support and cooperation are essential over the life of a project. Because issues requiring host government input can arise any stage of a project finance transaction, the quality and continuity of the government team responsible for the project is especially important in enabling the government to respond expeditiously and intelligently.

2. Sponsor. The other critical decision maker in a project financing is the sponsor. The sponsor is the party who identifies the project as a potential business opportunity, takes the lead in assuring that all of the necessary feasibility and preparatory work is done and provides or arranges for the financing of this work. If, after reviewing all the feasibility work, the sponsor decides to proceed with the project, it is generally the lead equity investor and arranges the project's debt finance. Governments may also be initiators or sponsors of projects which they identify as critical for economic development. This is often the case in infrastructure pro-

jects which the government initiates and supports with the participation of the private sector through concessions or other contractual arrangements.

3. Lenders. Lenders are generally sophisticated but conservative and cautious. Since the lenders rely on the cash flow and assets of a single project, they are ultra-sensitive to any fact that might interrupt cash flow or reduce asset value. As a result, they conduct extensive due diligence of the project and its risks and typically insist on back-up credit support, loan covenants and other legal arrangements designed to ensure that their loans will be repaid in all circumstances. Since the lenders provide the bulk of the funding, they have great bargaining power which means that there is often little room for negotiation on their basic demands for protection.

4. Engineers and Other Technical Experts. The input of engineers and other technical experts is critically important to the ultimate success of any project. This expertise is necessary to assess the basic technical feasibility of the project, provide the detailed engineering essential for construction, organize procurement, supervise construction activities, determine whether the project's completion tests have been met, and conduct and monitor the ongoing operation of the project.

5. Contractors. Major project financings require experienced and creditworthy contractors in order to ensure that the facilities are completed on time, on-budget and according to specifications. Failure of contractors to complete on time and/or on budget may require additional funding to be raised, and capacity and operational deficiencies resulting from

inadequacies in construction will diminish the project's revenue stream. These factors will impact debt service capacity and the rate of return on project equity.

6.   Providers of Credit Support. Because most lenders are reluctant to rely solely on the project's revenue stream as the source of repayment of their loans, they commonly require additional credit support. This support can be provided in a variety of forms from a variety of sources including: completion guarantees and overrun funding commitments from sponsors; guarantees and other commitments from the host government; credit and specific risk guarantees from multilateral institutions; commercial and political risk insurance; warranties from equipment manufacturers and various types of surety bonds and letters of credit.

7.   Purchasers and Users. The entities that use the project facilities or purchase output from the facilities are critical participants in any project financing because the payments that they make constitute the revenue stream which the lenders rely on for the repayment of their loans. As a result, lenders will careful assess the creditworthiness and reliability of these entities and, if they have doubts, may seek credit support for the payment obligations of the users or purchasers.

8.   Input Suppliers. The suppliers of inputs essential for construction and operation of the project include suppliers of major equipment that form part of the project facilities and the providers of the inputs needed to operate the facility. Deficiencies in major equipment and inability to supply needed

inputs will impact project output and performance and generally reduce the project revenue stream.

9. <u>Operator</u>. Operation and maintenance of project assets at a level that meets expected performance requirements and industry standards is essential if the project is to generate needed revenue on a sustainable basis. Operation and maintenance services can be provided by an independent third-party operator or by one or more of the other project participants. Lenders will sometimes appoint their own independent engineer to monitor the provision of these services.

10. <u>Advisors</u>. Virtually every project financing utilizes the services of specialized advisors, and the use of high quality advisors can often make the process of preparing and implementing a project more efficient and enhance the prospects of ultimate success. The type of advisors needed will vary from project to project, but it would not be unusual for a major international project to utilize the services of lawyers, engineers, financial advisors, risk and insurance consultants, environmental experts, human rights and community relations advisors, market and demand consultants and country and political risk advisors.

The large number of participants in a typical project financing means that a number of differing, and often conflicting, legal interests need to be considered and accommodated by the sponsor and its legal team.

D. Main Stages

Raising funds using the project finance method involves a series of interrelated transactions undertaken over a lengthy period of time and which require extensive preparation and complex documentation. As a result, a project financing generally unfolds in stages or phases. A common way of describing the various phases is to divide a project into pre-construction, construction, and operational periods.

1. <u>Pre–Construction Phase</u>. The pre-construction phase can be divided into three distinct subphases: a Pre–Feasibility Phase; a Feasibility Phase and a Preparation Phase.

a. *Pre-Feasibility Phase*. The basic purpose of this phase is threefold: (1) to determine whether there is a basic commercial or public service need for the project and whether it is consistent with overall sponsor and government objectives; (2) to define preliminarily the basic parameters of the project by considering alternatives, undertaking early stage conceptual design and cost estimates; and (3) undertaking limited studies to enable the sponsor to form a very preliminary opinion as to whether the project could be technically and commercially viable and whether funds could be raised for construction and operation. If the sponsors and/or government conclude that there is a reasonable chance that the project will be viable, they generally commit to provide funds to undertake more intensive feasibility work.

b. *Feasibility Phase*. During this phase, the sponsors are trying to make a definitive decision as to whether they should commit to the project and provide further funds to undertake the process of detailed project preparation. Typically, this stage involves hiring advisors and consultants to produce studies which provide the analysis to determine whether the project is feasible and to ensure that there is no fatal flaw that would prevent the ultimate success of the project.

The exact feasibility studies undertaken would vary with the nature of the project but the main activities usually undertaken in this phase include:

- technical engineering studies, including preliminary cost estimates;

- market studies to assess the project's ability to obtain needed inputs at reasonable prices and to sell the output or service;

- an assessment of the basic economic viability of the project;

- the preparation of a preliminary financial model for the project;

- a financial feasibility analysis to provide a preliminary assessment of the bankability of the project and its ability to raise funds;

- an analysis of the potential environmental and social problems that the project might create for the community in which it is constructed and operates;

- analysis of the political, legal and investment climate of the host country;
- reserve studies (for natural resource projects); and
- a risk analysis of the project.

Once the sponsors and/or government determine with a high degree of certainty that the project is viable and can be successfully accomplished, they agree to commit substantial additional manpower and financial resources for the more detailed preparatory work. The feasibility phase then morphs into the Preparatory Phase which builds on the feasibility studies already undertaken.

c. *Preparatory Phase.* The objective of this phase is to bring the project to the point where funds can be raised and actual construction can begin. This requires an intensification of some of the work begun in the feasibility stage and the initiation of major additional work. Specifically,

- technical and engineering work continues to produce detailed engineering and construction plans;
- decisions are made on the method of procurement and, if necessary, bidding documents are prepared;
- bids from prospective contractors will be sought if a competitive bidding process is being used;
- additional studies of environmental and social issues will be prepared to comply with host country and/or lender requirements;

- all permits and licenses needed to commence construction will be obtained;
- decisions will be made on how the project will be structured and managed;
- drafts of the basic project documents will be prepared;
- equity subscription, shareholder and other agreements involving the sponsor will be prepared;
- debt finance is arranged for the construction of the project;
- the project site is cleared and made ready for construction to begin; and
- if the site is remote, construction of access roads, utility services and temporary facilities for workers and utilities is undertaken.

Once the essential preparatory work is substantially completed and construction funding has been arranged, the construction phase can begin.

2. <u>Construction Phase</u>. During the early part of the construction phase, any unfinished preparatory work is completed (e.g. finalizing permanent funding to take out construction loans; refining the detailed engineering and cost estimates; and finalizing project documents). Once physical construction is completed, a series of completion tests are conducted to ensure that the facilities meet design specifications, operate at expected performance levels and enable the project to comply with any financial completion tests. Once it is certified that all

relevant completion tests are met, any construction period guarantees or other obligations made by sponsors or other parties are discharged and the periods for the validity of any warranties given by equipment suppliers or others usually begin.

The construction period is generally the riskiest phase of any project with the main risks being: (1) delayed construction and/or cost overruns; (2) inadequate funding to complete the project; and (3) non-completion or abandonment. Most long term permanent lenders for the project are reluctant to assume these risks and refuse to provide significant construction period funding. The institutions that do provide loans for construction will generally require some form of guarantee or other credit support. This means that sponsors and the contractor often need to assume most of the construction period risk. The sponsors do this through equity contributions, sponsor advances and loans, and completion guarantees or other support to construction lenders. The contractor also assumes substantial construction period risk in cases where there is a fixed price turnkey construction contract.

3. Operational Phase. During the operational phase, the focus of the host government, the sponsor and the permanent lender is on ensuring efficient management and operation of the project in order to create a sufficient revenue stream to pay operating costs, taxes, debt service and a return on sponsor equity. In addition, once construction has been completed and all completion and performance tests have been met, the permanent financing can be drawn down and used to repay construction

period loans and advances from sponsors and other construction lenders.

Once operation begins there is a shift in who bears the main financial risks of the project. Construction lenders have no continuing risks as their loans should have been repaid. Sponsor risk also decreases considerably as the risk of non-completion or abandonment is over and sponsor loans and/or guarantees have been repaid or extinguished. The main remaining risks for the sponsor are that its equity return will be lower than anticipated and/or its equity investment lost in the event that the lenders or the government seize project assets because of a default which leads to termination. On the other hand, permanent lender risk increases considerably as their funds have been disbursed and they generally become subject to significant financial risks for the first time.

E. Documentation

One of the characteristics of an international project financing is the complexity of the documentation. The documentation used will vary from project to project depending on a variety of factors, including the sector, the project structure, and the nature and source of finance. The following provides a list of some of the more common documents found in project financings which lawyers will be called upon to prepare or review.

Project Documents

- feasibility studies
- financial models
- agreements for advisory services
- joint venture or other organizational documents
- agreements among sponsors/shareholders/partners
- documentation creating the special project vehicle
- bidding and other procurement documents
- concessions or other similar agreements
- miscellaneous permits and licenses
- environmental assessments and permits
- government support or implementation agreements
- rights of way, land titling and other real property documentation
- construction contracts
- technology licensing agreements
- various bonding, insurance and surety documents
- input supply agreements
- offtake, user or tolling agreements
- advance payment agreements
- production payment or sharing agreements
- lease agreement

- operation and maintenance agreements
- transportation agreements

Finance Documents

- mandate or commitment letter
- preliminary term sheet
- confidentiality agreements
- offering memorandum
- loan agreements and related documentation
- bond issue, Rule 144A and traditional private placement documentation
- B–Loan participation agreements
- equity subscription agreements
- sponsor completion and overrun funding agreements
- guarantee agreements
- intercreditor agreements
- project account documentation
- documentation establishing security over project assets
- collateral trust account agreement
- documentation related to any derivatives used in the transaction
- general commercial and political risk insurance documentation
- closing documents and legal opinions

Not all of these documents are involved in every project, and the point of including this lengthy list is to illustrate the number and variety of documents that a project finance lawyer may be called upon to draft or review during the course of a major international project financing.

The documentation for a project financing is often grouped into broad general categories. This book will use two categories: Project Documents (encompassing both organizational and operating agreements) and Finance Documents (encompassing the documents relating to the loan agreement, credit support, security and intercreditor relations).

F.   Why Would a Sponsor Choose to Use Project Finance?

Project finance is a complicated, time consuming method of raising funds when compared with the simpler corporate or sovereign finance methods discussed previously, This raises the question of why would any entity choose to use project finance. This is a question that sponsors also must consider by evaluating the advantages and disadvantages for the specific project in question before embarking on a project financing.

1.   <u>Disadvantages</u>. The potential disadvantages include:

- complexity;
- the length of time that it takes to prepare, negotiate and document the financial arrangements;

- higher costs both in terms of both preparatory expenses and interest rate and other financing costs;

- restrictions on sponsor/SPV freedom of action resulting from lender contractual control; and

- difficulty in renegotiating and restructuring.

2. Advantages. There are a number of positive aspects of project finance that often offset the disadvantages for the sponsor. The three main advantages are the fact that:

- debt raised by an SPV may not appear on a sponsor's balance sheet which may enable the sponsor to expand its debt capacity by avoiding restrictions on additional borrowing in its existing debt instruments. This could be especially useful for smaller or less creditworthy sponsors or governments who would not be able to raise debt for the projects on their own balance sheets;

- a sponsor may be able to share risks with other project participants and reduce its exposure to risk that it would need to assume entirely on its own if using traditional corporate finance. This ability to share risks may be of special importance in very large projects; and

- the general diversity of lenders and frequent presence of MDB's and ECA's in major project financings provides a "halo" effect which may help make a project bankable by minimizing adverse host government action.

Any sponsor considering how to fund a major project must carefully weigh the advantages and disadvantages of project financing as compared with traditional corporate or sovereign borrowing. In the final analysis, whether it chooses to use the project finance method will depend on the size, nature and location of the project, the nature and extent of the project's risks and the sponsor's own creditworthiness and tax and accounting needs.

CHAPTER 2

THE ROLE OF LAWYERS IN A PROJECT FINANCING

A. Overall Staffing of an International Project

Since a multidisciplinary approach is required if major projects are to be successfully structured and implemented, project finance lawyers need to work in close coordination with experts from an range of other disciplines. The exact size and composition of the project team is determined by the nature of the project, but in most cases the core group should include members with engineering, financial and legal expertise. This core team would need to have ready access to specialized expertise in insurance, procurement, transport and logistics, project management, accounting, labor relations and personnel matters, and environmental, community relations and other social issues. The characteristics of an international project financing make it essential for all participants to devote adequate staff and resources to the project. It is especially important for the two key decision makers—the host government and the sponsor—to have independent, adequately funded, multidisciplinary teams to provide objective advice to senior government or corporate management officials at all stages of a project.

B. General Role of Lawyers

The nature and intensity of a lawyer's work varies depending on the project phase and the participant that is being represented. However, in all major international project financings lawyers play a critical role. By virtue of the fact that they help negotiate and draft all key documents related to the project, they are *ex officio* automatically involved in all key aspects of the project. This gives them a unique role and enables them to perform a coordinating function in addition to providing substantive legal input.

It should be kept in mind that no single attorney has the depth or breadth of expertise needed to provide adequate legal service to all aspects of a project financing. As will become apparent in the discussion in subsequent chapters, very specialized expertise is required to deal with such diverse areas as tax law, procurement law, construction law, loan agreement negotiation and advice on dispute settlement. It is, therefore, not surprising that the bulk of the legal work in connection with major project financings is provided by large international law firms that have the range of expertise required.

C. Legal Work by Phases of the Project

Although the nature of the lawyer's role varies with the phase of the project, each project is unique; and the work of the lawyer is not always neatly divided into sequential phases. Therefore, while the following outline of the work in each phase given below is typical, there are bound to be exceptions from these descriptions.

1.   <u>Pre-feasibility and Feasibility Phases</u>. The legal work in the pre-feasibility and feasibility stages is normally relatively limited and often related to preparing general assessments of the host country's investment climate, tax laws, and overall legal and judicial systems. In addition, the lawyer might be asked for a preliminary assessment of the laws relating to the sector in which the project might be undertaken and the regulatory agencies and rules that might impact the project. The objective of this analysis would be to identify any fundamental legal issue that might influence the decision of the sponsor to proceed with the project.

2.   <u>Preparatory Phase</u>. Once the project moves to the preparatory phase, the lawyer's work expands dramatically. Lawyers play a key role in:

- the bidding and procurement process;
- structuring the SPV and designing the overall legal structure of the project;
- conducting due diligence;
- obtaining needed permits and licenses;
- the drafting of all of the shareholder and sponsor agreements, the concession, the construction contract and other project documents;
- preparing drafts of information memoranda and offering circulars, loan, credit support and security agreements and other finance documents; and

• coordinating financial closings.

3. Construction Phase. The construction phase generally requires somewhat less intensive work from lawyers who will normally be using this stage to finalize any documents not previously completed and documenting and closing permanent finance if not already done in the preparatory phase. In addition, there are frequently contract issues that arise during construction which require legal attention. If a dispute review board is unable to resolve construction related disputes to the satisfaction of the parties, lawyers may need to become involved if the issue moves to another phase of the dispute resolution process.

4. Operating Phase. If all goes smoothly in the operating phase, the lawyer's role may be limited to what is basically a monitoring function. It would prepare a Monitoring Memo for its client containing, *inter alia*, a list of all reporting requirements and a summary of all loan agreement covenants that need to be complied with to avoid loan default. Unfortunately, operations do not always go smoothly; and the lawyers will find themselves involved in a various ongoing legal issues. These include: evaluating and opining on requests for waivers from the requirements of project and financial documents; dealing with events of default under the various agreements; inter-creditor issues; and agent bank requests for guidance in carrying out their responsibilities. In addition, most projects require renegotiation or restructuring at some stage and lawyers become involved in renegotiating loan agreements and other documents. Finally, differences among the parties are bound to arise over the life of a

major project and the lawyer will be involved in helping resolve disputes whether by negotiation, meditation, arbitration or court proceedings.

D. Project Side and Finance Side Legal Work

There are two distinct, but interrelated, substantive parts to the legal work for every project financing—the project side and the finance side. The project side work involves representation of sponsors, the SPV, contractors, offtakers and other parties to project agreements. It focuses on structuring the sponsor's interest in the project and the overall contractual framework of the project and the drafting and negotiation of the project documents. The finance side work involves conducting due diligence on behalf of the lenders, arranging and documenting the loans and other funding for the project along with the related credit support, security and inter-creditor arrangements. The two areas are interrelated and equally important in that the legal work on the project side forms the foundation for a bankable project which makes it possible to raise finance.

PART II

PROJECT PREPARATION AND STRUCTURING

CHAPTER 3

RISK IDENTIFICATION AND DUE DILIGENCE

Feasibility work, risk identification and due diligence are closely related activities undertaken in the pre-construction phase of a project. The object of the feasibility work is to enable the sponsors and/or government to determine with a high degree of certainty whether a project can be successfully implemented and whether they should provide the substantial additional funding needed for more detailed preparatory work. Risk analysis is generally done as part of the feasibility work and is designed to alert the project participants to the key risks to the success of the project. Due diligence is a term used to refer to the review that parties considering participation in the project undertake to ensure, *inter alia*, that: the feasibility studies are adequate; all key risks have been identified; adequate risk mitigation measures have been implemented; and the project documents work together to create a bankable project.

A. Risk Analysis

1. <u>Importance of Risk Analysis</u>. It is an axiom of international project finance that success depends on careful planning; and risk analysis is an essential part of the planning process. Sponsors, potential lenders and other interested parties all wish to avoid bearing excessive risk and look for ways to mitigate or transfer risk. As a result, they all engage in risk analysis before deciding to participate in a project. This means that the individual project and its potential risks are subjected to microscopic analysis—often with the aid of specialized risk analysis firms.

2. <u>Methods of Risk Classification</u>. Project risk analysts generally separate risk into broad categories for the purpose of identification and discussion of mitigation techniques. The precise categories vary depending on the nature of the project, and risks are often classified according to the point in the project cycle where they generally appear—e.g. pre-completion risks and post completion risks. There are many ways to classify risk, and an example of one general framework for risk classification is as follows:

- Project Preparation and Management Risks;
- Market Risks;
- Technical, Construction, and Operational Risks;
- Legal and Contractual Risks;
- Financial and Credit Risks;
- Political and Institutional Risks;

- Environmental Risks; and
- Community Relations, Human Rights and other Social Risks.

Identification of individual risks is project specific, and the analyst has to identify the various risks and then prioritize them by taking into account the probability of the risk occurring, the potential damage to the project and the ability to mitigate. The lawyer is, of course, responsible for identification of the legal risks and for suggesting ways to mitigate them. In addition, the lawyer is also involved in devising contractual methods of allocating, minimizing or avoiding other types of project risk.

3. <u>Risk Matrix</u>. Potential lenders to a project expect that a major effort will be made to identify all possible risks to the project, and this requires the various experts involved in the project to identify risks in their areas of responsibility. The results of these efforts are then reflected in a comprehensive risk matrix showing the key risks, their consequences for the project, possible mitigating measures and the party or parties responsible for bearing any residual risk. The preparation of a risk matrix is a standard part of a project financing, and every finance plan and Offering Circular or Information Memorandum should have an extensive section on risks and risk mitigation. (An example of a Generic Risk Matrix is found at Appendix 1).

B. Legal Due Diligence

The nature of the topics considered in a due diligence exercise will vary from project to project depending on the nature of the participants, the type of project and the host country concerned. However, in all projects the lawyer normally prepares a Legal Due Diligence Report for its client. The scope of such report will vary depending on the client (e.g. lenders as opposed to sponsors) but would commonly include analysis of:

- The basic legal framework and laws of the host country that might impact the project, including:

  - laws and regulations relating to inward investment;

  - laws, regulations and regulatory agencies governing the sector concerned;

  - tax laws and regulations;

  - laws and regulations relating to foreign exchange that might affect the ability to convert and transfer interest, dividends and other project distributions;

  - ability to obtain security over project assets and to enforce such security;

  - quality and independence of the host country judicial system;

  - dispute resolution issues including: available forms of ADR; choice of law and forum options; laws and treaties relating to arbitration; and willingness of the local courts to enforce arbitral awards.

- Analysis of the project's concession (or similar basic agreement).

- Analysis of all other contracts supporting the project and making it bankable. The due diligence in this area would consider such matters as (1) how the contracts work together to create and support the revenue stream and (2) the consistency of the clauses of the various contracts relating to such issues as force majeure, liquidated damages, and governing law.

- Review of the procurement process involved in the project to ensure that it was in accordance with applicable law.

- Review of all loan documents, inter-creditor agreements and security arrangements to ensure that, if there is more than one lender, there are no major differences in default clauses, covenants and other key clauses.

Legal due diligence is an ongoing process as some of the work can be done in the feasibility and risk identification phase while other aspects need to wait until the preparation phase when most of the key contracts and loan agreements are drafted. Since lenders' lawyers will need to review the key project documents to ensure that they are internally consistent and create the basis for a bankable project, they will need to wait until there are final drafts of these documents. (See Appendix 2 for a Generic Checklist of Due Diligence Issues).

C. Specific Due Diligence Issues

Several issues are often the subject of more focused due diligence. They include:

1. <u>Public–Private Partnership Arrangements</u>. Many governments lack the resources and/or the expertise to provide the infrastructure and other government services needed for economic growth. This has lead to increased use of public-private partnerships (''PPP's'') in which the private party uses project finance techniques to raise money and construct a project to provide services traditionally provided by the public sector, including economic infrastructure like roads, water and power and social infrastructure like hospitals and educational facilities. A lawyer involved in a PPP project needs to carefully review all of the basic PPP laws and regulations of the relevant jurisdiction and ensure that all documentation is designed to ensure conformity with these law and regulations.

2. <u>Environment, Human Rights and Community Relations</u>. Although multilateral development institutions have had guidelines in some of these areas for many years, the environmental, human rights and community relations impacts of international projects are now receiving increased attention. Projects are often delayed and even cancelled as a result of deficiencies in these areas. A project finance lawyer is likely to encounter these issues as due diligence and legal risk analysis is conducted and should ensure that the sponsors and other participants are aware of these issues and undertake extensive consultations with the local commu-

nities affected by the project to obtain their input before proceeding.

3. <u>International Investment Law</u>. Every international project financing takes place within the context of the broader principles of international investment law. The explosion in the use of bilateral investment treaties, the growth in international investment arbitration and the introduction of specialized treaties like the Energy Charter are all factors which may impact an individual project financing and which must be evaluated by the project lawyers as part of the due diligence stage.

4. <u>Use of Derivatives</u>. Most major project financings involve the use of derivative contracts to hedge various financial and commodity risks. A project finance lawyer would not be expected to be an expert in the details of the use of derivatives. However, she should have an elementary knowledge of the general nature of the most common derivative instruments and how they are used to reduce risk in project financings. The project finance lawyer should also be aware of the basic legal documentation for derivatives and some of the key legal issues involved in the intercreditor relations between lenders and hedge providers. (A brief summary of the use of derivatives in an international project finance transaction is found in Chapter 18).

5. <u>Investment in, and from, the BRIC's</u>. There has been a dramatic growth in natural resource and infrastructure investment in, and from, countries like Brazil, Russia, India and China. (the so called "BRIC's"). Many of these investments will involve project financing, and legal due diligence for these projects must include an intensive review of the

relevant laws of these countries. For example, in late 2009 new Tentative Measures on the Administration of Loans for Fixed Assets and Guidelines for Project Finance Business became effective in China and may impact how project financing is conducted in China.

CHAPTER 4

PROJECT PROCUREMENT

Procurement is the process by which the goods and services needed to construct and operate a project are obtained. When procurement is done well, it is taken for granted. When done poorly, it can cause major complications. It requires careful planning to devise an appropriate procurement strategy, and procurement issues vary from project to project. This chapter outlines some of the main legal issues in the procurement process.

A. General Procurement Principles and Methods

Procurement is primarily part of the technical and engineering work of a project. The key decisions in the process are generally made by engineers, including decisions on such issues as: how to organize the equipment, services and construction work needed for the project into appropriate procurement packages; the technical specifications to be established for the goods and services being procured; and how to evaluate the bids in case of a competitive process. There may be some attention to procurement in the feasibility stage, but the intense work is done in the project preparation phase where decisions are made on whether to have competitive bidding and, if so, the form of the bidding and the nature of the bid package. The lawyer's primary role is to ensure the legitimacy of the procurement process through strict compliance with any applicable procurement laws or regulations. Lawyers may also provide substantial input into the drafting of the bidding documents and advise on protests from unsuccessful bidders and other legal issues that inevitably arise during the bidding and bid evaluation process.

1.   Basic Objectives. The ultimate objective of any procurement process is to obtain goods and services for the project in the most economical and efficient manner. This generally means obtaining project inputs that meet the needed quality and technical standards at the least cost. An important secondary objective is to have an open and transparent process that establishes legitimacy in the eyes of the potential suppliers and the public.

2.   Methods of Achieving these Objectives. There are two basic options to meet these objectives. First, the process may allow the project sponsor to identify contractors, suppliers and other input providers on the basis of its own experience and to negotiate directly with them to secure the best price and quality. The second option is to require the sponsor to use some sort of public competitive bidding process. The first option is informal and not governed by any specific rules or regulations. It implicitly assumes that the profit motive will be sufficient incentive for the sponsor to obtain the needed goods and services in the most economical and efficient

manner, but it is not a public process and lacks transparency. The second option assumes that a more formal competitive process that is public and governed by specific rules and regulations is needed to meet basic procurement objectives.

Although there are some exceptions, it is generally believed that procurement for major projects is best done through some type of competitive bidding process where offers from several bidders are solicited, received and evaluated in an open and transparent process. Not only does this lead to the lowest cost but it establishes a legitimacy which is important for governments and sponsors who may face opposition to major projects. It is for these reasons that host governments generally insist on competitive bidding when public funds are used in the project or when the project provides certain types of public services and multilateral development banks insist on competitive procurement procedures when their funds are used in a project.

B. The Procurement Process

1. Selection of the Rules. The precise nature of the competitive process is generally determined by reference to rules or guidelines established by the host country concerned or by any multilateral organizations lending to the project. Each country will have its own public procurement laws, and the various multilateral development banks also have their own detailed procurement rules that may be applicable. This means that the procurement laws and regulations governing any particular project

will depend primarily on its location and the sources of its funding. For example, an international project financing partially funded by an MDB will be required to follow the MDB's procurement procedures for those goods and services financed by the institution. The exact procedures used for competitive bidding vary depending on the country or multilateral lender involved, and these procedures have subtle differences which make generalizations difficult. Therefore, the remainder of this chapter focuses on two areas: the basic stages of a competitive bidding process and some of the legal issues that arise.

2. Basic Stages. A typical sequence of the main actions that need to be taken in an international competitive bidding process is as follows:

- decisions on the nature of the bid packages;
- decision on the method of procurement;
- prepare bid documents (or use standard bid documents);
- advertise the project internationally in widely read publications and request indications of interest and qualifications of the interested party;
- conduct a prequalification process to limit the number of bidders to a small group of qualified firms;
- send bidding documents to the pre-qualified firms and request proposals from them;
- provide opportunity for bidders to ask questions on the bidding documents;

- bidders prepare response on the basis of bid documents;
- bidders submit proposals by the established deadline;
- evaluate responses;
- select the preferred bidder;
- negotiate contract with the winning bidder; and
- adjudicate protests (generally at any stage of the process).

C. Issues That Require Legal Input

1. General Issues. At virtually every stage of the competitive procurement process outlined above, issues may arise that require legal attention. They include:

- Which laws or regulations apply?
- Is there any conflict between host country procurement law and the requirements of any multilateral lenders participating in the project?
- Is a specific form of bidding required? If not, what methods of bidding should be used?
- Do the specifications and evaluation criteria provide for equality of opportunity among bidders?
- How much "negotiation" is permitted with the preferred bidder after the award has been made without undermining the legitimacy of the bidding process?

- What process should be used to resolve protests by bidders who feel they have been unfairly treated?

2.   Concessions. Projects involving a concession from the government raise unique issues because procurement takes place at two levels. At the first level the government grants a concession to procure the services of a concessionaire to undertake the project; and at the second level the concessionaire needs to procure goods and services to construct the project. Under the procurement policies of most MDB's, if there is competition at the level of awarding the concession, the concessionaire does not need to use a competitive process in securing inputs in connection with the project itself. Conversely, if there has been no competition in the award of the concession, the MDB policies would require a competitive procurement process at the project level for goods and services to be funded by the MDB.

In addition, bidding for concessions is significantly different than bidding for more traditional goods and services. The UNCITRAL Legislative Guide on Privately Financed Infrastructure Projects describes the differences as follows:

"Laws and regulations governing tendering proceedings often prohibit negotiations between the contracting authority and the contractors concerning a proposal submitted by them ... As a result of that strict prohibition, contractors selected to provide goods or services pursuant to traditional procurement procedures are typically required to sign standard contract documents provided to them during the procurement proceedings.

The situation is different in the award of privately financed infrastructure projects. The complexity and long duration of such projects makes it unlikely that the contracting authority and the selected bidder could agree on the terms of a draft project agreement [i.e. the concession]without negotiation and adjustments to adapt those terms to the particular needs of the project. This is particularly true for projects involving the development of new infrastructure where the final negotiation of the financial and security arrangements takes place only after the selection of the concessionaire..." (p. 67)

"... The final negotiations should be limited to fixing the details of the transaction documentation and satisfying the reasonable requirements of the selected bidder's lenders. One particular problem faced by contracting authorities is the danger that the negotiations with the selected bidder might lead to pressures to amend, to the detriment of the Government and the consumers, the price or risk allocation originally contained in the proposal. Changes in essential elements of the proposal should not be permitted as they may distort the assumptions on the basis of which the proposals were submitted and rated." (p. 86)

This means that special care must be taken when conducting the bidding process for concessions and that lawyers must ensure that any subsequent

changes made in the terms of the concession to
meet lender demands are of a limited nature and
would not undermine the integrity and transparency of the procurement process.

3.   Unsolicited Bids. Some countries permit unsolicited bids. This means that the government does
not initiate the project by seeking bids but is willing
to consider proposals from the private sector to
initiate a project. The rationale for allowing unsolicited bids is that the private sector may have ideas
or proprietary technology that the government had
not considered and that might benefit the economy.

However, many countries that accept unsolicited
bids subject them to some type of competitive process. Some put any unsolicited proposals they receive out to public bid so that other firms may
compete but give the initial unsolicited bidder a
substantial "preference" in the evaluation process.
Other countries use a process known as a "Swiss
challenge". In this process, once the unsolicited bid
is received, the government negotiates with the
bidder on the terms and conditions of the proposal
and prepares a draft concession if one is required.
Once the government and the bidder have agreed
on the project and its basic terms, the government
announces the project and gives others a chance to
offer better terms and conditions than the original
proponent had offered. If it receives better terms
from a competent challenger, it then gives the original bidder a chance to match the new terms. If it
agrees to match, the project is awarded to the
original bidder. If it declines to match, the project is
awarded to the challenger.

CHAPTER 5

STRUCTURING THE SPONSOR'S INTEREST IN THE PROJECT

Once the sponsors have made the basic decision to use project finance rather than traditional corporate finance, they will need to make additional decisions on how the project will be organized and structured. This will involve decisions in three main areas: (1) structuring the sponsors' interest in the project, including the legal form of the SPV and the chain of ownership from the sponsor to the SPV in the host country; (2) establishing the terms of an agreement governing the relations among the project owners; and (3) selecting the contractual arrangements and other techniques that should be used to structure the overall project.

A. Basic Considerations

There are several key factors that will determine the ownership structure of the project. They include:

1. Sponsor Objectives. The sponsors and other potential owners often have very different objectives and expectations which will determine how they approach negotiation of their role in the project. For example, some may want immediate tax benefits

from asset ownership; others may place a high premium on keeping project debt off of their balance sheet; some will want the most flexible management arrangement possible; others may be participating to profit from construction or equipment supply contracts while others become equity participants to obtain a preference in receiving output from the project.

2. Tax. Each sponsor will generally want a structure that creates the most favorable tax results for its own involvement in the project. Some may prefer an SPV form that allows for flow-through-taxation because it may allow project income, losses, credits, depreciation and other deductions to be reflected at the sponsor level and not the SPV level. Others may place priority on deferring taxation by the sponsor's home country and want to structure their chain of ownership to include off-shore entities located in countries that afford favorable tax treatment or give investors the ability to defer taxes on earnings. Tax considerations like avoidance of withholding tax will also influence the form in which the project sponsor makes its financial contribution to the project, the nature of the financial instruments used to make the investment and the country from which the funding is sourced.

3. Accounting. Sponsors often structure the SPV and the overall project so that the SPV's assets, liabilities and income statements are not included in the consolidated financial statements of the parents. An investor may seek to avoid consolidation because of large operating losses of a subsidiary entity or to keep debt raised by the SPV for the project off of its balance sheet.

4. Limited Liability. A structure that affords limited liability in connection with the risks inherent in an international project financing is of crucial importance to many sponsors. Corporate entities that provide limited liability for owners or parent entities are common in most countries, and a sponsor who wishes to minimize liability will want to utilize these entities to structure the project in such a way that its ownership interest is through a limited liability company.

5. Control and Management. A sponsor will also consider control and management issues associated with its participation in the project. For example, how does it want to exercise control over its investment in the SPV? what role does it want to play in the day-to-day operation of the SPV? and how can a sponsor achieve its management objectives while preserving bankruptcy remoteness for the SPV? Typically the most flexible management arrangements can be obtained by using a partnership or joint venture where management issues can be agreed among the parties by contract. By contrast, when a corporate form is used, many governance and control issues are mandated or regulated by host country corporate law; and there may be less freedom for the parties to adopt more flexible arrangements.

6. Bankruptcy Remoteness. In structuring the SPV, sponsors need to consider the fact that project finance lenders are concerned that the SPV might become involved in a bankruptcy proceeding and have to share its assets and revenue with other creditors. There are two potential types of insolvency risk that are of concern: (1) internal insolvency

risk caused by factors relating the project itself and (2) external insolvency risk related to the possibility that the SPV would somehow be drawn into a bankruptcy proceeding involving one of its shareholders. Because the lenders have done extensive due diligence on the project itself, they are generally willing to assume the risk of the internal insolvency of the SPV. However, they are unwilling to assume the external insolvency risk. Therefore, lenders (and the rating agencies) insist that the SPV be isolated from the consequences of a bankruptcy proceeding of other project participants; and sponsors need to structure the project so that the SPV is bankruptcy remote.

B.   Structuring the Special Project Vehicle

In structuring its interest in the project, a sponsor is faced with three basic decisions: (1) does it want to own its interest in the project assets directly or through an SPV? (2) if it uses an SPV, what is the best legal form for the SPV? and (3) what chain of ownership should be used to channel equity and other funding from the parent sponsor to the SPV in the host country and to receive dividends, interest and other distributions from the project?

1.   The Options. The precise options available for the nature of the SPV will depend in large part on host country business organization law. In most countries some or all of the following options would be available: unincorporated joint venture; corporation; partnership; and limited liability company. These options have differing characteristics that

produce different tax, accounting and control implications for the sponsors.

2. Selecting the Best Option. The structure ultimately chosen will depend on the on the interaction of the factors outlined above and the characteristics of the form of business organizations being considered, including:

- limited vs. unlimited liability;
- control and management issues;
- ease of transferability of interest;
- ease of making new contributions;
- ease of withdrawal of profits;
- protection of minority rights;
- level of disclosure required;
- ease of dissolution;
- avoiding the possibility that the corporate veil will be pierced;
- subjecting the sponsor to regulation or environmental liability;
- nature of asset ownership (direct vs. indirect);
- flow-through-taxation.

3. Most Common SPV Forms. The most common forms for organizing the SPV in international project financings are:

a. *Corporation.* Some type of corporate form that provides: limited liability; assets owned by the corporate entity; a common financing vehicle that may enable off-balance sheet financing; ease of transfer of ownership interests and relative ease in creating security over project assets. However, disadvantages include less flexible management, potential for double taxation and lack of flow through of tax benefits to shareholders;

b. *Partnership.* Some type of partnership which provides: more flexible management; flow-through taxation; partnership ownership of project assets; an entity for arranging finance and entering into contracts; off-balance sheet finance for the partners; and the possibility of limited liability for some of the partners. On the other hand, there must be a least one general partner with unlimited liability, partnership interests can be more difficult to transfer than shares in a corporation and negotiating the partnership agreement is often contentious; and

c. *Unincorporated joint venture* which provides: direct participant ownership of a proportionate share in project assets; several liability; management flexibility via contract; flow through of tax benefits with taxation at the co-owner level which provides flexibility for each participant to make it own accounting and tax elections. The potential disadvantages are: there is no common financing vehicle as each participant must provide its share of project costs from its own resources; it is somewhat more difficult to contract and to provide security over project assets; and each participant has unlimited liability for its own share of the project.

C. **Structuring the Chain of Investment**

In addition to selecting the legal form of the SPV, sponsors need to focus on the channel or chain of ownership that they will use to make funds available from the parent in the home country to the SPV in the host country and to receive dividends, interest and other distributions from the project. This involves complex domestic and international tax and accounting considerations.

1.   Objectives. It is common in international project and investment transactions to try to create a chain of ownership structure where the ultimate owner: has some form of limited liability with respect to the operational and financial activities of the entity in which the financial investment has been made; avoids consolidation of the accounts of downstream entities with its own financial statements; and minimizes withholding and other tax obligations.

2.   Methods of Meeting Objectives. These objectives are often best accomplished by some combination of the following: (a) having several tiers in the ownership chain; (b) mixing corporate entities with partnership entities; (c) using tax havens in the chain of ownership; and (d) characterizing returns from the project in such a way that minimizes tax liability and/or leads to a preferred accounting treatment. Determining the most advantageous structure that balances the various factors and competing interests of different sponsors is challenging, and the sponsor group often considers multiple options before making a decision on the location and structure of the entities in the chain between the home and host country.

D. Structuring the Relations Among the Owners

It is common to have an agreement governing the control of the SPV and the relationships among the main sponsors and others with an SPV ownership interest. Such agreement sets out the rights and responsibilities of each owner of the project entity. The precise form of the agreement would vary with the nature of the vehicle but would typically be an Agreement Among Shareholders, a Partnership Agreement or a Joint Venture Agreement. These agreements are collectively referred to as "the Agreement Among Owners" (or the "AAO") for the purposes of this chapter. Because participants often have different and conflicting objectives, many contentious issues can arise in the negotiation of the AAO. Some of the main issues that need to be resolved are as follows:

1. Financial Issues.

a. *Contributions of the Participants.* One of the most frequently encountered problems concerns the relative contributions of the participants to the project. They must agree on such basic issues as: the amount and sequencing of each owner's financial contribution; the form of the contributions (e.g. will they be in cash or in kind); and provision of personnel, raw materials, or other inputs to the project. In addition, issues may arise with respect to the valuation of participant contributions when they are made in the form of in-kind contributions or in different currencies.

b. *Willingness to Provide Credit Support.* A related area of negotiation is the extent to which each party participates in providing supplemental credit support for the project in addition to its equity contribution. Such support can be provided in a variety of ways including: supporting construction period funding through a guarantee, a completion/cost overrun agreement; a purchase contract for project output; an advance payments for project output; or a deficiency agreement to support the revenue stream.

c. *Profits, Reserves and Distributions.* The owners also need to negotiate and include in the AAO provisions dealing with a the calculation and division of profits and the method for making decisions on how much should be left in the venture for working capital, reserves or expansion and how much should be paid out in the form of distributions to the owners.

2. Management and Control Issues. These issues relate to such matters as allocation of management responsibility, division of voting rights and, in general, how decisions involving the project entity are made. Each participant will have specific management and control objectives with respect to the project entity and the project in general. In addition, the laws of the host country often play a role in determining who controls the project. For example, host country legislation may require local shareholders to have a controlling interest. In addition, special voting mechanisms (e.g. different classes of stock) are sometime established for decision making in specific situations of special importance to one or more of the participants.

In some projects, a party may have a conflict between its interest as a shareholder or partner in the project entity and its other interests in the project as a contractor, equipment supplier or off-taker. In such cases, the AAO may require the party to abstain from participating in any decisions affecting its interests or establish special voting majorities. A participant may wish to sell its ownership interest to a third party not involved with the project. To deal with such cases, the AAO will generally contain provisions which provide for pre-emption, buy-out or right-of-first-refusal to provide the original sponsors an option to retain control.

3. Checklist of Provisions of an Agreement Among Owners. Whatever form the agreement takes, it should be based on the objectives and expectations of the various participants and include provisions that deal with the problems noted above. There is no standard form, but the following checklist summarizes the issues that are typically included in the Agreement among Owners.

- Preamble identifying the parties and setting forth the purpose of the project.
- Legal nature of the SPV.
- Provisions on the amount, type and timing of each party's investment.
- Voting rights and other decision making mechanisms for the project.
- Nature of other credit support expected from each participant.
- The sharing of credit support obligations.

- Licensing of technology and know-how from participants.
- Training of local personnel.
- Pricing of inputs supplied by and outputs purchased by participants.
- Planning and decision making for expansion or alteration of the project.
- Appointment of the management of the project.
- Clauses dealing with the impact of changes in exchange rates.
- Procedures to mesh differing accounting systems.
- Arbitration and dispute settlement.
- Choice of forum and governing law.
- Effects of subsequent changes in law.
- Transfer and assignment of interests.
- Termination provisions.

CHAPTER 6

CREATING THE OVERALL STRUCTURE OF THE PROJECT

The third major aspect of structuring an international project is selecting the techniques and contracts that will be used to allocate risk, create and maintain the revenue stream, and serve as the basis for raising funds for the project. In this part of the structuring process, the focus is on how to deal with the basic concerns of the lenders.

A. Basic Lender Concerns

The main lender concerns relate to the repayment of their loans. Since debt provides the major portion of the funds raised for project financings, this means that the project needs to be structured to provide assurances to lenders that:

- the project will be completed even if its cost exceeds estimates;
- if for some reason it is not completed, all outstanding debt will be assumed or paid by a creditworthy party;
- when completed, the project will generate sufficient cash flow on a sustainable basis to meet

debt service obligations as long as the debt is outstanding; and

- if for any reason the project's operation is interrupted, there is a mechanism in place to ensure that the lender's debt service will continue to be paid.

There are a variety of techniques and contracts which are the fundamental building blocks of any project financing and which are designed to provide the lenders with the assurances that they need. These techniques are frequently used in combination which means that it is common for a project to have more than one of these building blocks as part of its structure.

B. Project Finance Techniques and Structures

A typical project financing will involve one or more of the following specialized techniques or structures that create and support the revenue stream generated by the project.

1. Contractual Credit Support. In a structure based on contractual support, lenders advance funds on the basis of a contractual commitment by a creditworthy party (or parties) for the purchase of project output or the use of project facilities. An advantage of this structure is that it enables the credit and financial strength of the purchasers or users to be utilized to provide assured debt service for the project. In essence, the purchaser or user becomes an indirect guarantor of debt service.

The most advantageous type of contract is one in which the purchaser or user is obliged to make a minimum payment sufficient to cover debt service. This type of contract could involve:

- the purchase of power from a power station in amounts and at a tariff level sufficient to generate revenues adequate to service debt (a Power Purchase Agreement);

- the use of a newly constructed pipeline under an agreement to ship a minimum amount of oil or gas through the pipeline to generate sufficient revenues to pay debt service (a Through-put Agreement);

- an agreement to use a refinery or an LNG regassification plant to process a sufficient amount of ore or gas to generate enough tolling revenue to service debt (a Tolling Agreement); or

- the purchase of the output of a mine at a price and quantity adequate to generate enough revenue to service the debt advanced to develop the mine (an Ore Purchase Agreement)

The various types of purchase contracts are discussed in more detail in Chapter 10. From the standpoint of the lender and its lawyers, the key to any form of minimum payment contract is the nature of the purchaser's obligation to pay. In other words, how firm is it? Under what circumstances, if any, would a purchaser be excused from payment? There a number of different types or purchase or user contracts that have different types of minimum payment purchase obligations, and one of the key aspects of legal due diligence is to assess the nature and strength of this obligation.

2.   Deficiency Agreement. A deficiency agreement is often used in conjunction with a minimum payment contract to cover circumstances where the project is not able to provide the agreed level of output at a price which yields revenue sufficient to service debt. Under a deficiency payment agreement, a creditworthy party agrees to pay the difference between the revenues generated by the project and the debt service requirements. The party agreeing to make the deficiency payment is, in effect, a guarantor of a portion of debt service and provides additional underlying security for the loans to the project. One common use of deficiency agreements involves pipeline projects where the potential users of the pipeline agree to put a sufficient volume through the pipeline to generate adequate revenue to cover debt service or to make up any deficiency in such revenue through direct cash payments. Such an agreement is called a throughput-and-deficiency agreement.

3.   Production Payments. Production payment financing is a specialized financing technique which is commonly used to raise funds for mineral and petroleum related projects. There are variations of this type of financing but all involve the same basic concept. A financial institution advances funds to construct a project based on an assignment of the sponsor's interest in an oil, gas or mineral reserve or an agreed share of the production from such reserve. The lender has no recourse to the sponsor, and the "debt service" is then recovered out of the

proceeds of the sale of the lender's interest in the reserve or production from the reserve. In short, the lender obtains an interest in the reserve in the ground (or in the output from that reserve in countries where such interests are not permitted) and uses this interest as the means to ensure repayment of the funds it has advanced. There are, however, obvious risks to the lender if the reserve is underestimated or if there are production and marketing problems. In such cases, the lender would have no recourse to the sponsor or other project participants and risk the loss of the funds it had advanced.

4.   Advance Payment. A related method of raising funds for energy and mineral projects is advance payment financing. A sponsor or other interested party makes an advance payment for output from a yet-to-be-developed project and enters into a contract to take the output when production begins. The funds are advanced to a separate entity that uses them to develop the project. If the project is successful, the party advancing the funds is repaid in kind or through the proceeds of the sale of the output from the project. However, this party bears the risk of loss of all or part of its advance payment if the project is not successful.

5.   Lease Financing. Capital intensive projects like power plants often generate significant tax benefits which are available to the owner of the capital asset, which is normally the SPV. These benefits could include tax credits, depreciation allowances and start-up losses. The project sponsors often structure the SPV as a flow-through-taxation entity in order to capture these credits and deductions to reduce their own tax liability. However, there are

cases where the sponsor cannot use the tax benefits. This means that the tax advantages associated with ownership might be lost unless they were transferred to another party whose tax position permitted it to make use of the available credits or deductions. A common method of making such transfer is through a lease arrangement in which the facility to be financed is owned by unrelated investors who can use the tax benefits and who are willing to lease the facility back to the SPV. The advantage of this type of financing is that the lessor is willing to share some of the tax benefits with the SPV by charging lease rentals that would be less than the SPV's borrowing costs. There are several types of lease financings including leveraged leases, financing leases and operating leases. Whether a particular lease financing is possible and beneficial to the sponsors depends on a complex set of tax, legal, financial and accounting factors that need to be carefully evaluated by experts in lease transactions.

6.   Project Accounts. Lenders will often seek assurances that the revenue stream will not be diverted or used in ways that would make it unavailable for debt service. One way to do this is through the creation of a series of project accounts designed to isolate the cash flow of the project and make it available for debt service on a priority basis. For example, in the case of a mining project in which output is sold abroad, the lenders might insist on offshore trust and require the purchasers to make payment to the trustee rather than the SPV in the host country. The trustee would then segregate in the trust account amounts sufficient to pay taxes, essential operating costs and debt service. Only if

all of these obligations were satisfied would funds be released to the owners of the project.

7. Hybrid Project Financing. Some of the sponsors of a major project may wish to arrange financing in the traditional manner on their own direct credit while other sponsors prefer to use project financing. The needs of both groups may be met through the use of an ad hoc, specialized financing facility which blends project financing with more traditional joint venture financing. The key feature of such a facility is the creation of a partnership composed of those participants who wish to fund their share of project costs through off-balance sheet project financing. The partnership would be one of the co-venturers, represent the sponsor/partners' individual and collective interests in the project and raise funds on the basis of contractual commitments to purchase output from the partnership.

8. Public–Private Partnerships. The concept of a public-private partnership was described in general terms in Chapter 3 as a contractual arrangement in which a private sector party is given a right to construct a project to provide public services that were traditionally provided by governments. The private party often uses project finance techniques to raise the funds needed for construction and implementation of the project. Public-private partnerships are commonly undertaken pursuant to a concession from the government or other public authority. Under the concession arrangement, the private entity is generally given a license to build and operate an infrastructure facility for the duration of the concession. It is expected to mobilize funding for the facility's construction,

oversee the construction and operate and maintain the facility using its own resources. The private participant would be entitled to the profits of the venture within limits established by the concession or host country regulatory regime.

A variety of arrangements are used to split ownership, risks and responsibilities between the private participant and the host government. They are best known by their acronyms, and some of the most common are:

- BOT (Build, Operate and Transfer). A private sector investor finances, builds and operates (but does not own) the project facility and transfers it back to the government at the end of the concession period.

- ROT (Rehabilitate, Operate and Transfer). This is a variation on the BOT scheme. A private party rehabilitates existing assets rather than building new ones and then operates, receives revenues and ultimately transfers back to the government.

- BOOT (Build, Operate, Own and Transfer). The project facility is financed, built, owned and operated by the private investor who transfers it back to the government at the end of the concession.

- BLT (Build, Lease and Transfer) The private participant finances and builds the facility but acts as lessor and leases it to a government agency for operation. At the end of the lease, the facility is transferred to the government agency.

PART III

PROJECT DOCUMENTS

CHAPTER 7

INTRODUCTION TO PROJECT DOCUMENTS

This chapter begins the examination of the three main categories of project documents typically found in a major project financing. The categories are concessions, construction contracts; and operating agreements. The discussion that follows emphasizes the need for careful coordination among these agreements and provides examples of why such coordination is necessary.

A. Integrated Nature of Project Agreements

The three categories of documents work in combination to help allocate risks among the participants and to create the revenue stream on which a project financing is based. In other words, the interaction of the project documents creates the foundation for raising finance for a major project. One of the key tasks of the project finance lawyer is to ensure that the terms of the agreements governing the actual operation of the project are drafted so that they are consistent and function in an integrated way. This is done by focusing on the categories of clauses common to the various agreements and ensuring that the consequences of an event that affects one contract will not have an adverse impact on other project agreements.

B. Relief Events: Reasons for Non–Performance

The need to synchronize project documents is illustrated by considering the various events or circumstances that may be used to excuse a party to one of the project agreements from its obligation to perform. These concepts are sometimes collectively referred to as "relief events" and include the following:

- *Force majeure*: an event or circumstance beyond the control of a party to a contract that adversely impacts its ability to perform its obligation under the contract.

- *Material adverse state action:* action (or omission) by a government that causes a material adverse effect on the project or the economic position of the affected party.

- *Hardship*: a change of circumstances that was not foreseeable, is beyond the control of any of the parties, upsets the economic or financial balance that existed at the time the contract was signed and causes undue hardship to one of the parties.

- *Imprevision*: a civil law concept which refers to a change in the economic or financial circumstances that makes a party's performance more difficult but still possible.

- *Frustration of contract*: primarily a common law concept that refers to a change of circumstances that occurs without the fault of any of the parties and which alters the nature of the contractual obligation and makes it incapable of being performed in the way that was called for in the contract.

- *Impossibility of performance*: an event occurs that makes it absolutely impossible for the party to perform its obligation under the contract.

- *Commercial impracticality*: a change of circumstances which means that, while performance of the obligation is still possible, it is no longer financially viable for the party to do so.

- *Material adverse change*: action that has a material adverse effect on the assets or business prospects of a project, the ability of one of the parties to meet its obligations or the validity or enforceability of project documents.

These are all very general concepts whose precise definition and application to a specific factual situation in a project financing is often the subject of legal controversy. The concepts may be interpreted quite differently in civil law and common law jurisdictions and lead to different results for the party relying on the concept. For example, in some civil law countries, the concepts of force majeure and imprevision may be embodied in administrative law or the civil code and automatically incorporated into a contract even though not specifically mentioned. On the other hand, under the common law, the concept of force majeure would not be implied and would need to be specifically addressed in the body of the contract. In addition, even in cases where a general concept is well understood and accepted by the parties, there are often significant differences in the way lawyers will draft the language of the clause containing the concept.

C. **Examples of the Need for Coordination**

1. Force Majeure Clauses. The concept of force majeure (also sometimes referred to as "FM") provides an example of some of the issues that can arise when a party to one of the project agreements tries to rely on one of the relief events noted above. The basic concept of FM is deceptively simple as it refers to an event beyond the control of a party to a contract that adversely impacts its ability to perform under the contract. Most project documents will have a force majeure clause that provides a basis for excusing an affected party from performance. This non-performance will likely have effects on the other project agreements which could prevent the SPV from performing its obligations under these contracts. This might subject the SPV to significant liabilities unless it was also relieved from these obligations by the FM provisions of these other contracts. To ensure this relief, the force majeure clauses of all of the project documents need

to be drafted and interpreted in a consistent manner.

However, when it comes to embodying the concept into a contract and/or interpreting the language of a force majeure clause, a number of issues arise. They include:

- What type of adverse impact does the event need to have on the party's ability to perform? Does it have to make it absolutely impossible or illegal to perform or is it sufficient that the FM event have a material adverse impact, create an undue burden or make it commercially impracticable to perform?

- Does the event have to be one that was "unforeseeable" or "unforeseen."?

- Does the force majeure event have to be unavoidable? If so, should the clause specifically require the affected party to try to avoid or mitigate the impact of the event?

- Must the party claiming force majeure give notice and/or provide evidence to the other party? If so, what are the requirements as to timing and form?

- How broad should the scope of the clause be? Should the clause divide the general concept of force majeure into political force majeure and natural force majeure and deal with them separately or should there be a single definition that covers both types of event?

- How should a project agreement deal with FM events occurring in other project agreements in the chain from concession, construction, supply, operation to ultimate sale? Should a force majeure event in one document automatically be a force majeure event in all project agreements?

Because the parties to the various project agreements may answer these questions differently, there are many variations of the FM clause which result in differences in the scope of coverage and preconditions for the existence of a force majeure event. For example, some clauses require the event to be foreseeable while others do not; some clauses require the affected party to take measures to avoid any adverse impact while others do not; and some clauses require the event to make performance impossible or illegal while others only require that the event have a material and adverse effect on the affected party's ability to perform. There is potential for similar differences in drafting and interpretation in connection with other key contract clauses which underscores why a project finance lawyer drafting or reviewing the various project documents must make a major effort to ensure consistency.

2. Consequences of Inconsistency in Force Majeure Clauses. Without coordination, it is possible to have differing interpretations or mismatches in FM clauses which can create major problems if the language is not made consistent. A classic case is where the FM clause in the construction contract is broader than the FM clauses in other project con-

tracts. This means that the contractor is able to claim force majeure in the construction contract with the SPV but the SPV is not able to claim relief under the FM clauses of the other project contracts such as the concession, supply or offtake agreement. This type of mismatch is of major concern to lenders, and it is the job of their lawyers to catch this problem in the contract due diligence process.

3. Liquidated Damages in the Case of Delay in Construction. Another example of the need for coordination of contract clauses involves a situation where there is a delay in construction of a power plant which is the fault of the contractor and not a result of force majeure which would excuse the contractor's delay. Under the EPC Contract, the contractor would generally be liable to the SPV for liquidated damages. Normally, the basic operational contracts would have commencement dates linked to the start-up date of the plant. If the facility is late in starting-up and the cause of this delay is not also a relief event under the basic operational contracts, the SPV also would owe liquidated damages to the power purchaser, the supplier and perhaps the government under the concession.

4. Coordination of Dispute Settlement Clauses. Each project agreement could conceivably have its own dispute settlement clause with a different governing law, a different resolution process and a different forum for hearing the dispute. This means that disputes involving the various interrelated documents might be brought in more than one forum and/or under more than one governing law due to differences in dispute resolution clauses in the various project documents.

CHAPTER 8

CONCESSION AGREEMENT

In most international project financings there will be some type of agreement between the host government and the SPV which establishes the basic terms and conditions that govern the implementation of the project. The agreement will typically: (1) grant the SPV a license or other right to carry out the project; (2) set forth the respective rights and duties of the government and the private sector participant; and (3) govern the overall operation of the project.

These basic terms and conditions may be included in different types of contracts with different names, including concession agreements, joint venture contracts, production sharing agreements, master agreements, implementation agreements, BOT agreements, PPP agreements, lease agreements, offtake agreements and licensing agreements. The terminology is often confusing which means that the lawyer must look behind the label to determine the specific terms and conditions governing the nature of the relationship between the host government and the SPV. The material in this chapter concentrates on concession agreements because they are the most common type of basic agreement.

A. Basic Legal Framework

The substantive content and the process for awarding concessions will be determined by the host country's laws and regulations, the nature of any specific law dealing with concessions and the regulations governing the sector in which the concession is granted. For example, the host country constitution may limit or prevent direct foreign ownership of an interest in certain sectors of the economy. A specific law for concessions may set forth general objectives, method of award, nature of government support and a list of topics to be covered in concession agreements. The regulations for the sector in which the concession is granted may also contain requirements which need to be incorporated into the concession. This means that in drafting an individual concession agreement the lawyers need to ensure that its provisions comply with basic host country laws and regulations.

B. Design of Individual Agreements

There is no universal, standard form of concession applicable to all projects as the terms of each agreement will be determined by the provisions of the basic law and a combination of factors peculiar to the country, sector, and nature of the project. Because negotiation of individual concession agreements can be costly and time consuming, some governments have developed standard form concession agreements for key sectors which they expect the private party concessionaire to accept. Despite great variation in terms and conditions of concessions, there are a number of matters which are dealt with in most concession agreements and which are set forth in a checklist in Appendix 3.

C. Potentially Contentious Clauses

Some clauses often lead to difficult negotiations between the Grantor government and the SPV Concessionaire. The remainder of this chapter identifies and discusses a few of these clauses.

1. Completion Date and Liquidated Damages. Concessions will generally establish a specific date for completion of the project and require the concessionaire to pay liquidated damages if the project is delayed beyond the specified date. In addition there will be provisions in the agreement identifying events or conditions that would postpone the completion date and excuse any obligation to pay liquidated damages for delay. There are often difficult negotiations over the type and scope of the events that would justify delay in completion and over the amount of the liquidated damages owing.

2. General Relief Events. Concessions generally contain one or more of the "relief events" discussed in the previous chapter. Four of them are discussed in this section.

a. *Material Adverse State Action Clause*. Under this clause, the host government would be required to compensate the concessionaire for losses suffered as a result of government action (or inaction) that adversely affected the operation of the project. Actions that might be covered include: expropriation; introducing a law that adversely affects the project; allowing competing facilities to be constructed; and failure to allow agreed tariff adjustment. Negotiations over the issues raised by the clause focus on the definition of what constitutes a material adverse action, the nature of any national security or other exceptions, the causal connection between the action and the loss suffered by the sponsor and the method of determining damages.

b.　*Hardship or Economic Balance Clause.* Many concessions and project agreements prepared by lawyers with a civil law background contain hardship or economic balance clauses. The essential elements of these clauses are: (1) a premise that the rights and obligations of the parties are based on the circumstances surrounding the contract at the time it is signed and the expectations of the parties as to how these circumstances might evolve over the life of the project; (2) a change in these circumstances or expectations that is not caused by a force majeure event; (3) the change was not foreseeable and was beyond the control of either of the parties; and (4) the change upsets the economic or financial balance that existed at the outset between the parties and causes undue hardship to one of the parties.

The consequence of the occurrence of the change of circumstances is that the parties are obligated to try to agree on a way to restore the economic balance. If they cannot agree within a specified time period, a notice of termination may be filed by either party. In addition, in some civil law countries, administrative law judges would have the power to restore the parties to a position of equity. Given the rather general nature of the concepts of hardship and economic equilibrium, there is obviously a great deal of room for negotiation in trying to define the nature of the change of circumstances that will trigger the clause, the meaning of economic equilibrium or hardship and what it takes to restore the balance.

    c. *Stabilization (or Change in Law) Clause.* Sponsors frequently seek assurances from the host government that the laws and regulations in place at the time the investment is made will not be changed to the detriment of the project. Such assurances were often furnished by a stabilization clause which provided that the concession and the project would be governed by the laws and regulations in effect at the time of the investment and that any subsequent changes in laws affecting the project would not be applicable. In other words, the law governing the project is frozen in time.

    Such a clause creates an inevitable conflict between the investor's desire to protect itself against a form of political risk and the government's insistence on its right to preserve its sovereign right to change its own laws. As a result of this conflict, more recent versions of stabilization clauses are sometimes limited in various ways. Common methods of restricting the clause have included: (1) narrowing the scope so that it only applies to laws in specific areas critical to the project such as taxation; (2) coupling a stabilization clause with a readjustment or renegotiation clause which requires the parties to try to agree on action to restore the project's original equilibrium; (3) permitting general changes in law that affect the overall economy or sector concerned but prohibiting any changes directed specifically at the project; and (4) permitting changes as long as the state agrees to compensate the investor for any damages caused to the project.

d. *Force Majeure Clause.* See Chapter 7 for a discussion of force majeure clauses and the need for careful drafting to prevent a force majeure clause in the concession from having unintended consequences for other project documents.

3. Termination. There are several ways that a right to terminate may arise which are summarized in the checklist in Appendix 3. Whatever the reason that gives rise to the right to terminate, the parties will generally try to keep the project operating if it has the potential to be profitable. They try to negotiate provisions in the concession that would permit continued operation by giving the lenders step-in rights and the right to designate a substitute concessionaire or by enabling the government to assume operation. However, to take account of the possibility that the concession will actually terminate and the project will no longer be operational, the concession will contain provisions for the government to take control of, and make payment for, the remaining project assets.

Even in cases where termination is caused by a default by the SPV/concessionaire, the lenders will expect the government to provide compensation to the SPV sufficient to repay their loans. The theory is that, if the government does not provide such compensation, it will be unjustly enriched as it has received a physical asset that was created using the lender's funds. This leads to difficult negotiations with the government over its obligation to compensate and on how to determine the amount of the its compensation (e.g. fair market value of the assets; going concern value; cost of the asset; or the amount of the outstanding loan balances).

4.   Waiver of Sovereign Immunity. Entering into a concession agreement would generally be considered a commercial activity under the restrictive theory of sovereign immunity which means that an explicit waiver of immunity from jurisdiction may not be absolutely necessary. Nonetheless, the concessionaire and its lenders will commonly seek a clause providing for an waiver so that a host government will not be tempted to raise an immunity defense in case it is sued.

5.   Dispute Resolution. Because they involve issues of sovereignty and national pride, the negotiations over the form, forum and governing law of dispute settlement can be contentious. From the host government's perspective, the ideal method would be to settle disputes in local courts in accordance with local law. However, the courts and legal systems in many countries have limited experience in dealing with investment and financial issues that arise in the context of major projects. In addition, some countries do not have an independent judiciary and their courts have developed a reputation for giving excessive weight to political rather than legal considerations in rendering decisions. For these reasons, concessionaires will often seek dispute resolu-

tion clauses providing for matters arising out of the concession to be decided by arbitration in a neutral country according to the law of a jurisdiction with more experience in dealing with commercial and financial issues. See Chapter 21 for a more detailed discussion of the various options for dispute settlement.

D. Specific Lender Interests

At some stage, lender concerns will need to be considered by the host government and the concessionaire. In conducting due diligence, lenders and their lawyers pay special attention to the terms and conditions of the concession agreement to ensure that it is bankable. "Bankable" in this context, means that the concession agreement contains provisions that, *inter alia*, enable lenders to protect their interests in the project and ensure full repayment of their loans in the event of termination. In addition, if a multilateral development institution is involved in lending to the project, it will review the document to ensure that all of its own policies are accommodated.

The precise concerns of the lenders will vary from to project to project. However, terms that a lender would generally like to see in a concession for a project financing include:

1. Cure Rights and Step–In Rights. Cure rights would give lenders the right to take action to cure a default before circumstances arise that would enable one of the parties to terminate the agreement. Step-in rights would give lenders the right to step

into the shoes of the SPV/concessionaire and assume all of the rights of the SPV under the concession, including those needed to run the project in the event that the concessionaire was removed or unable to perform its obligations.

2. Adequate Compensation in the Event of Termination. Lenders will carefully review the agreement to ensure that it contains provisions requiring payment of compensation by the government that provides the SPV with sufficient funds to repay all of the lenders' outstanding loans to the SPV in the event of termination. Even though the government would have control of the assets, governments generally resist assuming such large obligations since one of the main purposes of granting a concession is to relieve the government of the financial burden of funding the project.

3. Security Interest in SPV Concession Rights. Lenders would also insist on a provision that makes it clear that they would be able to acquire a security interest in the SPV's assets and rights under the agreement as part of the security package for the project. The rights and assets that they want secured include not only the physical facilities but the intangible concession and concession rights.

4. Assignment of SPV Concession Rights. In order to exercise its step-in rights effectively, the lenders may also need the right to assume the concession and/or assign it to a third party who would operate the project in lieu of the defaulting private sector concessionaire. Therefore, they generally seek provisions giving them the right to take over the concession or to direct its assignment to a third party without prior approval by the govern-

ment. Such provisions are naturally resisted by the government as it wants to retain control over who operates the project and is reluctant to allow any assumption or assignment without its consent.

5. Amendment Approval Rights. Because the terms and conditions of the concession are so important in creating a bankable project, lenders generally try to have the concession include a clause that prevents any amendment of the concession by either the government or the concessionaire without lender consent.

6. Direct Agreement. The lenders are not a party to the concession and have no privity of contract with the government to ensure their ability of enforce lender rights under the agreement. Therefore, the lenders often seek a direct agreement with the host government in which the concession based obligations of the government benefiting the lenders are clearly spelled out and made directly enforceable against the government.

7. Dispute Resolution. For the reasons noted in Section C.5 of this chapter, lenders have preferences with respect to the dispute resolution clause. They generally prefer provisions that require that the government and the concessionaire resolve their differences through arbitration in a neutral forum outside of the host country using the governing law of a jurisdiction with a history of dealing with financial issues.

Note: See Appendix 3 for further information on the topics generally dealt with in concession agreements.

CHAPTER 9

CONSTRUCTION CONTRACT

The importance of the documentation and execution of the construction of any project is obvious as mistakes in the construction phase can put the entire project at risk. This chapter deals with some of the issues which the general project finance lawyer should be aware of in working with construction law specialists.

A. Main Types of Construction Contracts

There are three main types of construction contracts: (1) a fixed price contract based on a lump sum for all of the work covered by the contract (the "lump-sum" contract); (2) a type of fixed price contract where the payment to the contractor is based on an engineer's estimate of the quantities of the various items of work specified in the contract and a fixed unit price for each specified item (the "unit-price" or "measure-and-value" contract); and (3) a contract where the payment to the contractor is a reimbursement of the actual costs incurred by the contractor plus a fee for the contractor's services (the "cost-plus" contract).

B. Type of Contract Used in International Project Financing

The contract that is most commonly used in international project finance transactions is a fixed price turnkey contract known as an Engineering, Procurement and Construction Contract or simply the EPC Contract. A fixed price *turnkey* contract is a type of EPC contract where the employer expects the contractor to provide a completed project which can begin operation simply by turning a key to the completed facility. Under this type of contract the contractor receives a fixed amount for its services even if the actual total cost of the project exceeds the lump sum price that has been agreed in the contract. With some exceptions, the employer expects the contractor to assume responsibility for: design, procurement and construction of the project facility; all construction period risks; and cost overruns.

C. Standardization of Construction Contracts

Because international projects generally involve participants from different countries who may be operating under different regimes of construction law and practice, there have been major efforts to provide standard forms of construction contracts. The best known and most commonly used group of standard contracts for major international projects are produced by the International Federation of Consulting Engineers which is known as "FIDIC", its French language acronym. FIDIC has a broad international membership and has produced several standard form contracts for use in different types of international projects. The most relevant for the purpose of international project financings are the "Conditions of Contract for EPC/Turnkey Contracts". (the so-called "Silver Book") and the "Conditions of Contract for Design, Build and Operate Projects" (the "DBO Contract"). A standard contract like the FIDIC Silver Book is a good starting point for the drafting of construction contracts for international project financings.

D. Parties Involved in the Construction Process

The construction process for major international project finance transactions traditionally involved three key parties—the Employer or Owner; the Contractor; and the Independent Engineer.

1. <u>Employer</u>. The Employer (sometimes called the "Owner") is the party who initiates and signs the contract with the contractor, establishes basic design and performance requirements, and often provides specific design specifications and drawings to the contractor. The SPV generally serves as the Employer in an international project financing.

2. <u>Contractor</u>. The Contractor is the party who carries out the contract according to its terms. In international project financings, there is generally a single contractor (or a consortium of contractors) that enters into the contract with the Employer. However, in some cases the Employer may chose to

enter into separate contracts with a number of individual contractors who provide different components of the project construction (e.g. civil works and mechanical works).

3. Engineer. Major projects generally involve an engineering firm which acts as the project Engineer and performs a variety of technical tasks including: project design and detailed engineering; prepare procurement packages; participate in the adjudication of the bids received; administer the construction contract; supervise the construction; certify progress payments; determine if completion tests have been met; and help mediate and resolve construction related disputes. In many construction contracts, this three-key-party approach has evolved into a process where the two main parties are the Employer and the Contractor with the formal role of the Engineer changed to that of "Employer Representative". In addition, lenders will often appoint an Independent Engineer to help them assess the technical aspects of the project, conduct technical due diligence and monitor construction from a lender perspective.

E. Main Legal Issues in Construction Contracts

The main legal concern is how construction period risks are allocated between Employer and Contractor. There are some general industry practices that try to provide a fair and equitable balance of risk that are reflected in standard documents like those produced by FIDIC. However, there is no universal standard for risk allocation. These issues are subject to negotiation between Employers and Contractors, and a number are discussed in the remainder of this chapter.

1.   <u>Type of Contract</u>. The threshold issue is what type of contract should be used. The SPV and its lenders will generally favor a fixed price turnkey contract. On the other hand, a contractor generally prefers a unit price or cost plus contract and will build a premium into its quoted price to compensate for the added risks it is assuming under a fixed price contract.

2.   <u>Responsibility for Defects in Project Design</u>. A key issue is which party should be responsible for design defects that adversely affect project performance. Employers often supply design and other specifications to contractors which suggest that they should bear some responsibility. However, the Employer wants to pass the design risk to the Contractor even in cases where the Employer's specifications and drawings are used by the Contractor, and the Contractor naturally wants to avoid assuming the risk under these circumstances. The general practice is that the contractor is responsible for design defects on the theory that it should review any employer material and adopt it as its own.

3.   <u>Extension of the Completion Date</u>. On-time completion of the facility is critical as the other key project documents generally plan their commencement dates and cash flow forecasts from the date that the construction is completed. Thus, any delay in construction has a negative ripple effect throughout the project which affects cash flow and project economics. To provide some mitigation from these

adverse consequences, construction contracts generally impose liquidated damages on the contractor for each day of delay. In order to minimize the need to make liquidated damage payments, the contractor will negotiate for extension of time for completion due to events beyond its control such as force majeure or Employer requests for variation in the nature and scope of the work. In the event that delays are granted under the terms of the construction contract, the project lawyers must ensure that provisions for similar periods of delay are automatically reflected in other project documents so that the SPV will not be liable for delay damages under the supply, off-take and operation agreements.

4. Determining when Construction has been Completed. It is also critical to know exactly when a project is deemed to be "completed" because a number of key commitments and obligations are tied to the completion date. For example, shareholders of the SPV may have provided guarantees which continue in effect until completion; commencement of the effectiveness of other project agreements may be tied to completion of construction; and various warranties may not commence until project completion. Construction contracts have elaborate tests and procedures to determine exactly when a project is deemed to be complete. Tests include: mechanical completion (specifications are met); substantial completion (performance tests are met); and financial completion (project demonstrates that it can meet financial tests).

5. Role and Types of Liquidated Damages. Liquidated damages ("LD's") are a way of determining the amount of damages payable as a result of a

breach of contract which is based on an estimate of the approximate amount of damages rather than an actual *ex post* determination of the precise amount of damage. The amount of the liquidated damage is agreed in advance by the parties and specified in the contract before the occurrence of any actual breach. Liquidated damage clauses used in construction contracts generally require a contractor to pay LD's to the employer in two circumstances: (1) unexcused delay in completion and (2) failure to meet performance standards.

The delay LD's are generally calculated and paid on the basis of the number of days that the project is delayed beyond the completion date specified in the contract. Performance (or "buy-down") LD's are calculated differently. Performance LD's result from the fact that a project is designed so that the project facility performs at a level that will generate a revenue stream sufficient to repay the debt that has been borrowed for the project. If the actual performance is less than anticipated, the amount of revenue generated is reduced and the level of debt that can be repaid on a sustainable basis is reduced. Therefore, performance LDs are used to enable the SPV to prepay (or "buy down") a sufficient percentage of the debt to reduce the principal to a level when it can be serviced on a sustainable basis at the reduced performance level.

6. Adjusting or Reopening the Fixed Price. When a fixed price contract is used, Employer and the lenders can use the contract price as a basis for financial planning and determining how much finance will need to be raised for the project because

the contractor is required to assume responsibility for cost overruns. Therefore, the Employer will be reluctant to agree to broad price adjustment clauses. The contractor will, however, negotiate for adjustments in price resulting from force majeure and other events beyond its control; and there may be circumstances where the contractor is entitled to an increase in price and/or additional time to complete the construction. The SPV and its lawyers should ensure that any exceptions to the general practice that the contractor bears all the additional costs are clearly understood and carefully spelled out in the contract.

7. Payment Procedure. The most common payment procedure for construction contracts involves (1) an advanced payment to the contractor to provide funds for start-up costs such as mobilization and (2) a series of progress payments as work proceeds and various milestones are met. It is also common for the Employer to withhold a certain percentage of each progress payment as ''retainage'' which is put into an account and kept until completion to create a fund that can be used to correct any problems in construction. Issues that frequently arise in connection with payment include: the currency of payment; incentive or bonus payments and Employer's desire to have a bond or letter of credit from the contractor to ensure return of any advanced payment if the project is for some reason terminated before completion.

8. Methods of Assuring that the Contractor Performs as Expected. In an effort to ensure satisfactory contractor performance, construction contracts often create a system of incentives for high per-

formance (e.g. a bonus for early completion) and couple this system with provisions for penalties or compensation to those parties who suffer loss from failure of the contractor to perform as expected. Methods of providing such incentives and/or compensation include:

- performance bonds;
- other types of surety bonds;
- liquidated damages;
- letters of credit;
- warranties of design, materials and workmanship;
- retention payments;
- contractor parent or affiliate company guarantees;
- contractor indemnities;
- joint and several liability among contractors in a consortium;
- contractor direct guarantee to the lender;
- set limits on contractor liability at high amounts;
- security for the advance payment; and
- cure and/or step-in rights.

9.   The Force Majeure Clause. Virtually all construction contracts will have a force majeure clause which may excuse contractor performance and extend the project completion date. There are often negotiations over the precise wording of the clause as contractors want as broad a definition of force

majeure as possible to minimize liability while employers prefer narrowly drawn clauses to keep pressure on the contractor for on-time completion and to maximize liquidated damages. (See Chapter 7 for additional discussion of force majeure clauses).

10. <u>Special Dispute Resolution Measures</u>. Given the nature of the construction process for complex projects, it is common to have a large number of technical disputes arise between the employer and the contractor. It is in the interest of all parties to have disputes resolved quickly and efficiently, and the construction industry has developed the concept of a Dispute Review Board (or Dispute Adjudication Board) as an intermediate stage between negotiation and arbitration. It is designed to resolve disputes involving the technical issues that often arise during construction; and its members tend to be engineers or others with suitable expertise in the construction industry. The decisions of the board are not binding on the parties if either of them expresses dissatisfaction with the opinion of the board. In case of such dissatisfaction, the party may proceed to arbitration after a mandatory attempt to settle the dispute amicably.

CHAPTER 10

OPERATING AGREEMENTS

Once construction is completed, the main documents that govern the actual operation of most projects are: the concession; an offtake agreement; a supply agreement; and an operation and maintenance agreement. Concession agreements were considered in Chapter 8, and the purpose of this chapter is to examine the legal aspects of the other operational documents with an emphasis on the offtake agreement.

A. Offtake Contracts

There are two main ways that a project generates income: selling output under a purchase contract or charging for the use of project facilities under a user contract. For convenience, these two types of contracts are often combined and considered together under the generic name of offtake contract. This convention is used in this chapter.

1. <u>Wholesale and Retail Contracts</u>. The ability of a project to generate continuous sales or services is essential if the SPV is going to receive sufficient revenue to service its debt. An offtake contract with either a single purchaser or user or only a few creditworthy purchasers or users is a common

means of generating this revenue stream. These contracts are sometimes called wholesale offtake contracts.

There is another type of project financing where the lenders do not rely on a single (or a few) purchase or user contracts to create the revenue stream. These are projects where the SPV sells its product or service into the marketplace to a broad group of purchasers or users. Examples of such projects include toll roads, airports, ports, and other types of public-private partnerships. In the case of these merchant or retail project financings, the lenders do not focus on the terms and conditions of a single purchase or user contract for assurance that their loans will be repaid but on estimates of overall market demand for the project's output.

2. <u>Types of Wholesale Offtake Contracts</u>. There are several types of wholesale offtake agreements used to support project financings. The type of contract will vary by sector: power purchase agreements in the power sector; throughput and deficiency agreements for oil and gas pipelines; and tolling contracts involving smelters and other process related facilities. The different types of offtake agreements have different supply and purchase obligations which provide varying degrees of credit support for the lenders. Various short-hand names are used in the project finance field to describe the nature of the purchaser's payment obligations and the seller's obligation to supply. These names and a summary of their generally accepted meanings are:

a. *Hell-or-High Water*. Under this type of contract the purchaser must make payment "come hell or high water" (i.e. in all events) even if the project is not operating and the seller is unable to deliver the product or service;

b.   *Take-or-Pay*. A take-or-pay contract requires the purchaser to make payment even if it does not need the project's output or service and does not take delivery (i.e. it either takes delivery or pays). In traditional take-or-pay contracts the seller must have the capacity to produce and deliver before the purchaser's obligation to pay arises.

c.   *Take-and-Pay, Take-if-Available, and Take-if-Offered*. These contracts are similar in nature and generally require the purchaser to take delivery and make payment (even if it does not need the output or service at the time) as long as the project is able to provide the output or service.

d.   *Throughput and Deficiency*. These contracts are used in pipeline projects where shippers agree to ship enough oil or gas through the pipeline to generate sufficient revenue to service debt and pay essential operating costs. In the event that it does not meet this obligation, it would be required to make a "deficiency payment" to meet any shortfall in revenue.

e.   *Tolling*. Tolling agreements are used in refining, smelting or other projects that process raw materials where the user provides the raw material and pays a toll for processing services.

3.   Lender Preferences. The best type of contract from a lender's standpoint is one in which the purchaser or user agrees to make an unconditional minimum payment sufficient to service debt even in circumstances where the facility is not capable of

supplying output or services. The purchaser or user becomes, in effect, the guarantor of the debt and might be willing to assume such a one sided obligation if it has a great need to use the facilities or obtain output on an exclusive basis. Even though they are desirable from a lender standpoint, these types of contracts are difficult for most purchasers to accept. As a result, a more common form of minimum payment contract obligates the purchaser to make the agreed payment only if the project is operational and can supply the output or service. This means that the lender has less assurance that its debt service will be covered by payment under the contract and that it may need to look to other sources such as deficiency agreements, debt service reserve accounts, and guarantees in order to receive debt service when the project is not operating.

4. Reviewing Offtake Agreements. Each type of contract has a different division of obligations between seller and buyer/user which the lawyer must carefully analyze during the due diligence process. The key issues to be considered are: (1) the nature of the SPV/seller's obligation to supply; (2) the nature of the purchaser's obligation to take output from the project and/or make payment to the SPV; and (3) the circumstances that might excuse the SPV or its purchaser from their obligations. In addition, lawyers need to consider whether measures are available to compensate for a drop in revenue in the event that one of the parties is unable to meet its obligations under the offtake contract and the revenue stream is interrupted. The answers to these questions will determine the amount and quality of credit support provided by

the offtake agreement for the loans to the SPV for the project.

5. The Capacity Charge Concept. The structure of the tariff or purchase price set forth in the offtake contract will vary with the sector involved and the nature of the goods or services being sold. A common type of purchase contract used to support loans is the power purchase agreement (or "PPA"). Under these agreements the tariff structure used might be a fixed price tariff or one based on a combination of capacity and energy charges.

Under the capacity/energy charge type of tariff, the aggregate price for the power is primarily a combination of capacity charges and energy charges. The capacity charge is based on an agreed level of plant capacity that must be made available and covers basic fixed costs including debt service, taxes, insurance and other fixed operating and maintenance expenses. The energy charge is related to the amount of power actually supplied and is based primarily on fuel costs and other variable operating costs. When the agreed capacity is made available, the purchaser under a PPA must pay the capacity charge even if it does not take power and is excused from this obligation only in limited circumstances specified in the contract. Because the capacity charge covers debt service, lenders prefer tariff arrangements with capacity (or similar) charges because it helps insulate the project from inadequate demand.

An "availability payment" is an example of a similar concept. Under an availability payment structure, payment is made as long as the project is available for use and meets a certain standards of performance. An example is a toll road where the government makes an availability payment to the SPV/Concessionaire as long as the road is open and meets specified minimum standards

6. Price Adjustments. It is common in offtake agreements to establish an initial price and, at the same time, a formula for adjusting the price over the life of the project. The adjustment is normally based on changes in fuel or other input costs, foreign exchange rate movements, interest rate changes or inflation. Any changes in these variables would then be passed on to the purchaser in the form of an increased price, and the purchasers' increased payments would protect the value of the revenue stream for the lender.

However, lenders and their lawyers should beware of overestimating the protection that such escalation provides in protecting the revenue stream for debt service in extreme circumstances. The best example of the dangers of misplaced reliance on escalation clauses is the case of adjustment of tariffs denominated in local currency for depreciation of such currency against a foreign currency in which the loans for the project must be repaid. If the depreciation is substantial, the required adjustment in the tariff for the sale of output may be so large that the purchaser and/or its end consumers will resist paying the higher local currency tariffs which were designed to protect the foreign currency value of the revenue stream. A classic example of a case where such currency-change escalation clauses in power purchase agreements did not provide the intended protection occurred in Indonesia as a result of a depreciation of the Indonesian rupiah during the Asian financial crisis in the late 1990's.

B. Supply Agreement and Operation and Maintenance Agreements

Supply and Operation and Maintenance Contracts work together with the Offtake Agreement to generate and maintain a project's revenue stream. The SPV must have a continuous supply of essential inputs in order to produce the output to be sold to generate the revenue to repay the debt. Likewise, if the project facilities are not operated and maintained efficiently the project's ability to produce a steady revenue stream will be compromised. Even though they are equally important to project success, they are not considered in as much detail as the other project documents. The focus of this book is on basic concepts, and many of the main issues relevant to supply and O & M contracts have been introduced in connection with the discussion of concessions, construction contracts and offtake agreements. Supply contracts have many similarities to offtake contracts, and O & M contracts raise many of the same issues that were discussed in connection with construction contracts.

Supply and offtake agreements raise similar issues as they both are purchase and sale agreements. The SPV is the seller under a project's offtake agreement and the buyer under a project's supply agreement, and a take-or-pay offtake contract and a supply-or-pay supply contract are similar in nature. While these agreements are not mirror images of each other, they have a number of related terms such as duration, definitions of force majeure, and price adjustment clauses; and the issues discussed above in connection with offtake contracts with respect to the type of contract, the nature of purchaser and seller obligations, lender preference, due diligence and price adjustment are also applicable to supply contracts.

The situation is somewhat different in the case of Operation and Maintenance (O & M) Contracts. There are several options for providing operation and maintenance services to a project, and this leads to a greater variety of possible contractual arrangements. For example, these services could be provided under a single O & M contract with a sole provider or they could be disaggregated and supplied by different providers under a series of contracts. Also, the services might be provided by independent parties under a third party O & M contract or by the SPV, an affiliate of one of its shareholders or another project participant (e.g. a manufacturer who provides maintenance in connection with equipment that it supplied).

Whatever option is used, many of the concepts discussed in Chapter 9 in connection with construction contracts are also applicable to O & M contracts as the provider of O & M services has a role somewhat similar to that of the contractor. Issues with respect to type of contract used, risk allocation, performance standards, incentives and penalties arise in both types of contracts. The SPV will want to transfer as much performance risk as possible to the O & M operator and have a fixed price contract, a narrowly defined force majeure clauses, and penalties for poor performance. The operator will, like the contractor, prefer some time of cost plus contract, try to minimize the amount of performance risk it assumes and seek broadly defined relief events, loosely defined performance standards and limits on its liability.

PART IV

FINANCING DOCUMENTS

CHAPTER 11

ARRANGING FINANCE

Once the sponsors have determined that there is a good chance that lenders will find the project to be bankable, how do they go about raising and documenting finance? This is the general question dealt with in this and subsequent chapters as the focus turns from project documents to the actual loan transaction and its spin-off legal issues.

A. The Concept of Bankability

The topics that have been considered in previous chapters have dealt with those aspects of a project financing that combine to make a project bankable. "Bankability" is a fuzzy concept without any precise definition. In simplest terms, it means that: the project's economics are sound; it is structured in a way that is acceptable to potential lenders; and the lenders will be willing to make loans to the project. However, it is a subjective and not an objective standard; and the bankability of a robust well prepared project may vary with such factors as conditions in the financial markets, developments in the country where the project is to be located, and the quality and creditworthiness of the various participants. Thus, a project that is considered bankable in Country A might not be bankable in another country or even in country A at a later date if market conditions have changed. Moreover, a project that one type of lender is willing to finance may not be acceptable to another category of lenders.

B.   The Process

At some stage fairly early in the project preparation process, the main sponsor will begin considering how it should raise the finance needed to construct the project. Depending on the size and complexity of the project, it may also hire an outside financial advisor to assist. Work will be undertaken in a number of inter-related areas that are all prerequisites to arranging finance for a major international project. These areas include:

- a review of the project's technical feasibility studies to obtain information on cost estimates, expenditure schedules and the local currency/foreign exchange breakdown of these expenditures. This information will then be used to determine total funding needed in local and foreign currency and as input for constructing a project financial model;

- creation of a financial simulation model for the project as an essential tool to run the sensitivity analysis and alternative funding scenarios needed before final decisions are made on the financial issues related to the project. The model is used as a decision making tool throughout the life of the project;

- a procurement survey to determine the alternative sources of the equipment and services needed to construct the project and to assess the potential sources of export credit finance;

- a preliminary survey of potential sources of funding. The survey would assess: the capacity of each source for the country and sector concerned; and the comparative cost of funds from each source along with possible grace periods and maturities, currencies available and non-financial terms and conditions;

- an assessment of the potential debt capacity of the project based on preliminary financial projections;

- a determination of the most feasible debt-to-equity ratio for the project based on an assessment of the project's expected cash flow and the potential security and back-up credit support for the debt;

- the development and testing of a series of alternative financing plans;

- selection of the types of lenders that would be the most appropriate for the project and creation of a general strategy for approaching these lenders;

- the preparation of background material on the project needed for approaching potential lenders;

- approaches to various lenders to explain the project, test the level of interest and develop a short list of potentially interested lenders; and

- selection of one or more of the interested lenders and begin work with them on the loan documentation process.

The sponsor will be conducting this work at the same time as it moves forward with the completion of the other key tasks in the project preparation phase. There will inevitably be a period of iteration and adjustment as a result of the interaction between the various factors involved in putting the final project structure and finance plan in place.

C. Axioms and Basic Principles

There is no standard method or source of financing for major international projects as the finance plan for each project must be tailored to the needs and creditworthiness of the project and the country in which it is located. However, there are several axioms or general propositions that are widely applicable when creating a finance plan for an international project. They are:

1. No Standard Method. The sources of finance will generally be different for each project. There is no set pattern and a variety of factors which vary from project to project will determine the final mix of financing.

2.　Blending. Projects are generally funded by blending different sources and types of finance to fund different stages and components of the project (e.g. mini-perm or construction finance vs. permanent longer term finance; and export credit finance for major equipment purchases)

3.　Diversity of Lenders. It is common for international projects to involve (a) several different types of lenders including international and host country commercial banks, multilateral development banks, bilateral development institutions, export credit agencies and (b) a variety of credit support providers including commercial and political risk insurers, credit and specific risk guarantors, and hedge providers.

4.　Changing Market Conditions. The amount of funding available from private sources is constantly changing with market conditions, and the amount and percentage mix of finance available from the various sources to fund international projects will vary over time as markets change.

5.　Differences in Risk Tolerance. The goals and risk tolerance of the various lenders differ as private sector lenders are more risk adverse and profit oriented while official or public lenders tend to be less risk adverse and have development and social goals.

6.　Role of Public Sector Lenders. The largest potential sources of finance are the private commercial bank and capital markets as opposed to public or official sources of finance like multilateral development banks and export credit agencies. However, private sector funding can be volatile and unreliable as market conditions change, and it tends to be concentrated in more creditworthy countries. Although smaller in amount, public sector funding often has a catalytic effect that makes private funding possible and is also more readily available in less creditworthy countries.

7. <u>Debt/Equity Tension</u>. There is a tension between the sponsors and the lenders as to the debt/equity ratio. A project's debt-to-equity ratio is used to express the amount of debt relative to the amount of equity in a project (e.g. a $100m project with $80m in debt and $20m in equity has a debt/equity ratio of 4:1). The ratio will vary from project to project depending on such factors as the sector, the country, the quality of the participants, financial market conditions and the strength of any off-take agreement. A project with a high debt/equity ratio is said to be highly leveraged.

8. <u>Minimizing Refinancing Risk</u>. Sponsors generally try to avoid substantial refinancing risk by seeking loans with long maturities. When relatively short maturity debt (e.g. a mini-perm loan) is used to fund long term projects, all or a portion of the principal may mature before it has been fully amortized with funds from the project's revenue stream. This means that the borrower must arrange for new debt to refinance the outstanding principal amount of the shorter-term loan. If market conditions at the time of the refinancing are favorable, this may not be a problem for the project. However, it may be difficult to refinance at reasonable cost in poor market conditions with adverse consequences for project cash flow.

D. Basic Types of Finance

There are three basic types of finance used in project financing: equity; debt and mezzanine (or hybrid) finance. They have different levels of risk, different methods of receiving returns on investment, different ways of exercising control over the recipient of the funds and different legal rights in bankruptcy.

1. <u>Equity</u>. The providers of common equity (or the shareholders) are the owners of the project. They provide the risk capital for the project and receive their income primarily through dividends and potential capital appreciation. They control the SPV through the exercise of their voting rights which should enable them to control the Board of Directors. In short, the essential characteristics of common equity funding are:

- It determines ownership and control;

- It is permanent finance with no maturity;

- It bears greater risk but has greater potential reward;

- There is no assured repayment of the funds invested;

- There is no assured return on the funds invested;

- There is no contractual relationship;

- It does not add to the debt service burden;

- It cannot be rescheduled; and

- It the last category of finance to receive payment in bankruptcy.

The amount of equity provided will vary from project to project but the typical range would be 20–30% of the total cost of the project.

2.   <u>Debt</u>. The providers of debt funding for the project (i.e. the lenders) have a contractual relationship with the borrower through the loan agreement and not an ownership interest as the case of the shareholders. The lenders receive their income or return from the project in the form of interest rather than dividends or capital appreciation. They have no ownership or voting rights but may be able to exercise varying degrees of control through contractual conditions in loan documents. Debt may be secured through liens on project assets which may give it a preferred position in the event of bankruptcy or unsecured which means that the lender is a general creditor of the SPV for bankruptcy and other purposes. Finally, unlike equity, debt may be subject to rescheduling or refinancing. The lenders generally assume less risk and lower return in exchange for a more predictable contractual return. As in the case of equity, the percentage of debt in a project's finance plan will vary; but the typical range would be 70%–80% of total project cost.

3.   <u>Mezzanine</u>. Mezzanine capital (or hybrid finance) is any form of finance that ranks below senior debt but above common equity in seniority. It has a mix of the equity and debt characteristics outlined above and includes: preferred shares; subordinated debt; and convertible debt. Typically, mezzanine finance provides only a small percentage

of project funding and is often used to provide stand-by or contingent funding obligations in the form of subordinated debt provided by sponsors.

E. Nature of Equity Investor and Lender Concerns

For the most part, the concerns of the providers of the various types of funding will be similar. They will all be concerned with the basic economic and financial soundness of the project. In addition, they will want to ensure that the project is completed on time and on budget and that the revenue stream which is the source of their debt service and dividend payments is created and maintained as expected. They will also all be concerned with country and political risk, devaluation risk and potential environmental risk and liability.

However, shareholders and lenders also have some unique concerns which may need to be accommodated in devising a finance plan for the project. For example, they often differ on the on the debt-to-equity ratio as shareholders want to provide as little equity as possible to maximize the potential returns on their investment while lenders want as much equity as possible to ensure strong shareholder commitment and to increase their debt service coverage ratios. Shareholders will resist providing completion and overrun funding guarantees while lenders will often require them.

For lenders the prime concern is the certainty of payment of interest and principal at every stage of the life of their loans while shareholders may have made their investment for strategic business reasons and be able to wait longer to receive their returns. Lenders will insist on including measures in the loan agreement and in other finance documents to enable them to control the actions of the SPV and to take security over all project assets while the shareholders may see this as a reduction in their flexibility to manage the project. In the final analysis, however, it is the lenders who generally prevail when their interests diverge with those of the providers of equity. Debt finance constitutes the majority of the funding for most project financings which means that satisfying the concerns of the lenders is often the most critical part of creating a viable finance plan for a project.

CHAPTER 12

MAIN SOURCES OF FINANCE

A variety of sources are available to fund international projects, and the objective of the sponsor and its financial advisor is to blend the available sources together to create the most appropriate finance plan for the project. This chapter outlines the main sources.

A. Sources of Equity Finance

The bulk of the equity for international project financing is provided by the project sponsors. Lesser amounts are sometimes provided by other project participants (e.g. the contractor, equipment supplier or offtaker), multilateral institutions like the International Finance Corporation, bilateral government institutions, and specialized private sector infrastructure funds. Occasionally the host government provides equity either in cash or in-kind. In addition the project itself may provide "equity" for construction through cash generated by those parts of the project that have become operational prior to 100% completion of the entire project such as part of a toll road.

B. Sources of Senior Debt Finance

There are two broad categories of debt finance: private sector sources and public sector sources. It is common for finance plans for international project financing in emerging markets to have a mix of these sources.

1.   Private Sector Sources.

a.   *Commercial Banks.* In times when the financial markets are liquid, commercial bank loans are generally available for sound projects in most countries. The banks have staff experienced in evaluating project financings and are able to structure loans in a flexible way to help meet the needs of an individual project. They can provide construction, mini-perm and permanent finance; drawdowns can be tailored to meet the project's need for cash and to avoid negative carry; and commercial bank funding is available in a variety of currencies. Most banks have quick internal decision making and loan approval processes; bank loans can be amended or restructured relatively easily due to the use of agent banks and steering committees; and a credit rating is not always required.

In spite of these many advantages, commercial bank loans have some problematic characteristics. Interest on commercial bank loans is generally floating rate which can make financial planning difficult over the life of a project. While this risk can be hedged using the interest rate swap market, hedging increases transaction costs and involves counterparty risks. Cross border lending by commercial banks is very sensitive to financial market and political developments which means that it is a fickle source of finance. Traditionally, maturities on commercial bank loans have been shorter than those on other major sources of finance for international projects. Finally, commercial bank loan agreements generally contain very restrictive covenants which some sponsors may consider an unnecessary intrusion on managerial autonomy; and the bank lenders generally insist on substantial security over all project assets.

b. *Capital Markets.* The world's capital markets are huge and enable borrowers to utilize a great variety of instruments to raise funds from a broad universe of investors ranging from individuals to large institutional investors. Public bond issues can provide long maturities at fixed rate in a variety of currencies with few restrictive covenants and generally no requirements for collateral or security over project assets. In spite of these advantages, a number of factors have limited greater use of the capital markets to fund international project financings. These factors include: proceeds of the loan are generally disbursed in one lump sum which creates a negative carry problem for the project; they are an unreliable source of finance for international projects as they are very sensitive to market conditions and country creditworthiness considerations.; capital market issues generally require a rating from one of the credit rating agencies; interest rates tend to be higher; and public bond issues are difficult to renegotiate or restructure because they involve so many different ultimate investors.

c. *Other Private Sector Sources*. Major institutional investors like insurance companies and pension funds occasionally provide significant amounts of long term fixed rate funding for high quality projects in politically stable countries. In rare cases, private sector infrastructure funds and long term supplier credit will provide relatively small amounts of debt.

2. Public Sector Sources.

Multilateral and bilateral public sector institutions also provide funding and support for project finance in emerging markets. These institutions fall into three main categories: multilateral development banks, export credit agencies and bilateral development institutions. This section describes these groups in general terms; but, because they are numerous, no attempt is made to analyze the programs of individual institutions.

a. *Multilateral Development Banks*. Multilateral development banks (or "MDB's") are international organizations created by treaty whose shareholders are governments and whose loans are designed to support economic and social development. There are roughly twenty of these organizations of varying sizes with the best known being the World Bank, the European Investment Bank and the main regional development banks. Most lend primarily to governments, but MDB's (or their affiliates) are also able to provide assistance to international project financings in a variety of ways including the provision of equity and debt funding, credit and specific risk guarantees, and technical assistance.

The MDB's are a countercyclical source of debt funding that is relatively insensitive to conditions in the private financial markets due to the fact that they are owned by governments that donate funds to the institutions or indirectly back the MDB capital market borrowings through callable capital obligations. The major MDB's provide two basic types of finance: (1) market based or "hard" loans funded primarily from the proceeds of borrowings in the international capital markets and (2) "soft" loan finance funded primarily out of donations by member governments. Soft loans are available only in lower income countries and have very low concessional interest rates and very long maturities.

Most MDB's can lend at either fixed or floating rates and the interest charged on their market based lending is related to their own cost of borrowing in the international markets. Maturities and amortization schedules can, within limits, be tailored to project needs and can be in the 10–15 year range with longer maturities sometimes possible. The MDB's are generally less sensitive to the country and political risk of their borrowing members and have somewhat different standards of creditworthiness than private lenders. This means that their funding can be used to fund construction and may be available when private funding is not. It is relatively easy to amend loan and project documentation and often possible to obtain additional funding for the project from the MDB lender if needed.

In spite of these advantages, MDB funding has characteristics that sometimes deter sponsors from seeking finance from these institutions. All MDB policies with respect to its development goals must be followed, including very strict environmental and social policies that can delay project implementation and result in the imposition of restrictions on project operations. International competitive bidding is generally required for procurement using MDB funds, and the bank's evaluation, appraisal and internal approval process can be lengthy. Finally, while MDB's generally try to be accommodating to their borrowers, they have historically refused to participate in loan rescheduling, claiming preferred creditor status; and they require negative pledge clauses in their loan documentation.

b. *Export Credit Agencies*. Export credit agencies ("ECA's") are lending institutions created by many developed and developing countries to provide loans, guarantees, interest rate equalization subsidy, and political risk and credit insurance for the purpose of promoting exports from the agency's home country. ECA funding is an important source for major international projects as it is often available when private sources are not lending and has a somewhat higher tolerance for political and sovereign risks than private sector lenders.

The financial terms and conditions of most ECA lending is governed by a set of OECD guidelines (the OECD Arrangement on Officially Supported Export Credits) adhered to by most major exporting countries (but not China). The Arrangement establishes rules for the pricing, fees, maturities and other terms of conditions on the financing by those

ECA's that adhere to the guidelines. ECA funding can be fixed rate and the currency of ECA loans are generally denominated in the currency of the exporting country. The level of the interest charged by each country is based on a "Commercial Interest Reference Rate" for the country which is, in turn, based on the government bond yields for the currency of the loan. The Arrangement requires that, in addition to the interest on the loan, the ECA charge a premium for credit risk to cover the risk of non-payment. This premium or exposure fee is determined through a process set forth in the Arrangement which sets a Minimum Premium Rate which can vary considerably from country to country. There is also a special Annex X to the Arrangement which deals with the terms and conditions applicable to project finance transactions. It provides for more flexible and favorable amortization schedules than those applicable to non-project finance transactions which enable the repayment profile to match more closely the anticipated revenue stream. Specifically, loan maturities can be up to 14 years, principal can be repaid in unequal installments and flexible grace periods are permitted.

While ECA funding may be generally available in large amounts on favorable terms to help fund equipment and other services for major projects, there are some limitations on its use. The bulk of the procurement needs to be from the country that provides the loan which restricts the potential benefits of international competitive bidding. ECA financing is limited by the OECD Arrangement to 85% of the cost of the goods or services being financed which means that the other 15% needs to come from some other source. In addition, the premium for credit risk (or exposure fee) that must be charged in addition to interest can, depending on the country in which the project is located, make the overall cost of the loan relatively expensive.

c. *Bilateral Development Institutions*. Many countries have development agencies providing loans and other assistance to the private sector projects. These include OECF of Japan, KfW of Germany, OPIC of the US, various Chinese government financial institutions, BNDES of Brazil, the Development Funds of Abu Dhabi, Kuwait and Saudi Arabia, and the 15 bilateral institutions that that belong to the Association of European Development Finance Institutions (EDIF). Each institution has its own unique programs which can be found on its website.

C. Sources of Mezzanine Finance

Since mezzanine finance is a hybrid which blends some of the characteristics of equity finance with those of debt, its main sources are some of the providers of equity and senior debt discussed above. While sponsors would rarely provide senior debt to the SPV, they often provide subordinated debt either as quasi-equity mezzanine finance or in the form of a stand-by commitment to cover any potential cost overruns. Some of the MDBs' private sector lending affiliates may provide subordinated debt, preferred equity or other forms of mezzanine funding. Other sources include the various bilateral development agencies who are members of EDFI and a limited number of specialized infrastructure funds.

D. Other Sources of Finance

a. *Carbon Finance*. In recent years a new type of funding has emerged for projects that produce significant environmental benefits. This method is made possible by the provisions of the Kyoto Protocol to the UN Framework Convention on Climate Change which provides a way for entities in the developed world to help fund environmentally sound projects in emerging markets. The Protocol establishes binding emission reduction targets for countries that adhere to the protocol and then creates various market based mechanisms to help counties and their corporations meet these targets. One of the options is the Clean Development Mechanism (the "CDM") which provides a method for governments and private entities to help fund certified projects by purchasing Carbon Emission Reductions (or "CER's") generated by the project. The CER's can then be used to satisfy obligations under the Kyoto Protocol. The Executive Board of the CDM has established a procedure for certifying projects that generate net environmental benefits and for calculating the CER's for each project. The CER's can they be sold by the project in the market to generate revenue to help fund the project or support debt raised for the project.

Looking at the program from a project finance perspective, the CER's generated by a project can be seen as part of the project's output which can be sold in the market to either fund part of the project (e.g. by selling CER's in the forward market to generate funds to help fund construction) or by selling the CER's generated by the project on an ongoing basis to form part of the revenue stream used to repay the project's debt. The potential buyers of CER's include private companies, governmental entities, financial institutions, carbon market trading houses and carbon funds like those established by the World Bank.

b. *Islamic Finance.* Islamic finance is a source of funding for international projects that must comply with *shariah* principles. This compliance is ensured by review conducted by *shariah* boards in Islamic financial institutions, some national *shariah* boards or the Accounting and Auditing Organization for Islamic Financial Institutions. (AAOIFI). The main advantage of using Islamic finance is that it enables a project sponsor to tap the large pool of funds in the Middle East—especially for major projects in that region.

In spite of some similarities with project finance (e.g. both involve asset based financing), it has often proven difficult to combine Islamic finance with traditional project finance. *Shariah* principles prevent Islamic lenders from collecting interest on their loans which requires them to use other methods to earn a profit on their investments. They do this by using techniques that enable them to (1) provide capital through partnership type arrangements in return for a share of profits (or losses) or (2) purchase ownership of the asset being financed and then sell or lease the asset to the SPV and earn a return by a price markup or lease payments. These methods may not always be possible in complex project financings and may create problems for traditional lenders who may require first priority security interests in the same project assets. In addition, the fact that funding from an Islamic financial institution needs to be reviewed by a *shariah* board to determine its acceptability creates an added level of uncertainty; and the use of *shariah* compliant finance together with non-Islamic finance may raise issues as to the governing law of the project. Finally, there are a relatively limited number of *shariah* compliant instruments, maturities on Islamic finance tend to be shorter than those typically sought for major project financings, and the use of *shariah* based derivative and hedging products to mitigate project risks is still in the early stage. While these problems are not insurmountable, they create added complexity and make it more difficult for Islamic finance to be used in the same project along with traditional commercial bank, export credit and multilateral bank funding.

CHAPTER 13

THIRD PARTY CREDIT SUPPORT

Ideally, sponsors would create a project that is bankable without the need of extensive third-party credit support. They do this by careful mitigation and allocation of project risks and by careful preparation and structuring of the project and the project documents. However, these measures are not always sufficient to convince potential lenders that a project is bankable; and lenders will often require additional credit support for their loans. This chapter considers the various instruments and techniques often used in combination to provide the needed support.

A. Types of Third Party Risk Mitigation and Credit Support

1. <u>Insurance</u>. Insurance companies may be willing to assume (for a premium) risks that lenders are unwilling to accept; and to maximize the benefits of insurance most major international project financings will have an independent insurance advisor to help identify key risks and design the most appropriate insurance package for the project. Various forms of insurance are standard in major project financings to cover commercial and political

risks, and the most important types as discussed below.

2. Direct Guarantees. Various types of third party guarantees are often used to cover project risks and provide credit support to lenders. A direct guarantor agrees to back the obligation of a project participant if that participant does not fulfill a monetary obligation or perform as agreed. This could take the form of a guarantee of the payment of debt service or guarantee of performance that affects the revenue stream such as an obligation to purchase project output.

3. Standby Letter of Credit. In cases where there are concerns about a project participant's creditworthiness or ability to perform, standby letters of credit are often used as secondary payment mechanisms to provide credit support. For example, a bank might issue (for a fee) a letter of credit at the request of the EPC contractor to provide assurances to the Employer of the contractor's ability to perform a specified obligation under the EPC contract. If the contractor does not perform, the Employer beneficiary would be able to draw on the letter of credit by providing evidence of non-performance. Examples of the use of letters of credit to provide support in project financings include backing liquidated damage obligations, debt service reserve obligations, equity contribution commitments and various contractor obligations.

4. Surety Bonds. The main function of a surety bond is to provide assurance to entity A that its dealings with entity B will be backstopped by a bonding company which is assumed to be a creditworthy party. Surety bonds are commonly used to

provide credit support for payment or performance during the procurement and construction phases of a project and are sometimes used during the operational stage. They include: bid bonds to cover cases where a successful bidder fails to enter into the relevant contract; performance bonds to cover cases where the contractor does not properly perform; warranty bonds to cover cases where the contractor fails to deliver on a warranty; and retention bonds provided by a contractor in lieu of the Employer retaining a portion of each progress payment. Surety bonds provide support that is similar to that provided by guarantees, insurance and letters of credit but there are subtle legal differences in these instruments that project finance lawyers should be aware of when reviewing them as credit support measures.

5.   Warranties. A warranty is type of assurance or guarantee given by a contractor, equipment supplier or other party providing goods or services to a project which states, in essence, that the product or services provided will meet all agreed specifications and performance standards or, it they do not, that the warrantor will remedy the defect and/or pay compensation for damages caused by the inadequate performance.

6.   Derivatives. Most major projects use the private sector financial markets to obtain hedges using derivatives to deal with interest rate, currency and commodity risks. The most common instruments used are interest rate and currency swaps and the commodity forward and futures markets. See Chapter 18 for further discussion of the use of derivatives in international project financing.

B. Commercial Insurance

This section focuses on insurance of commercial risks associated with international project financings and considers a number of insurance related issues from the perspective of potential lenders to the project.

1. Lenders' Interest. The basic interest of the lenders in insurance matters is to ensure that any insurance proceeds are used to repair damage and keep the project in operation or to repay debt. In furtherance of this interest, the lenders also will seek broad insurance coverage for the project and the perfection of a clear legal right for lenders in any insurance proceeds. Measures which help establish clear lender rights include: assignment of the policy to the lenders; establishment of a security interest in the insurance proceeds; making the lender a co-insured party; creating a right for the lenders to get paid directly by the insurance company as a loss payee; and ensuring that the lender has the ability to "cut-through" a host country insurance company policy to have direct access to an international reinsurer.

2. Scope of Coverage. International project financings involve the purchase of several different types of insurance. The exact scope of coverage and the standard insurance package generally required by lenders will vary from project to project and with the stage of the project, but the typical risks covered by insurance during construction and operation are as follows:

Construction Period Risks

- contractor all risk which protects against loss during construction irrespective of the cause, including loss caused by defective design, materials or workmanship;

- delay in start-up of the facility which protects against the consequences of loss of revenue resulting from insured loss or damage during construction;

- marine all risk for equipment shipped for the project which protects against loss during transit irrespective of the cause;

- marine delay in start-up which protects against the consequences of loss of revenue resulting from insured loss or damage during transit; and

- third party liability which provides coverage relating to liability for bodily injury and property damage.

Operational Period Risks

- operator's all risk which provides protection against loss or damage caused after operation has begun irrespective or the cause;

- machine breakdown (if not covered in operator's all risk policy);

- business interruption which protects against revenue loss resulting from insured physical loss or damage at the owner's site and, in some cases, may also cover loss of revenue resulting from damage at the site of a customer or supplier; and

- third party liability which provides coverage relating to liability for bodily injury and property damage.

In recent years, insurers have become more creative in helping to mitigate project risks, and have developed new types of coverage for project finance, including increased coverage of political risks in international projects. Although extensive use of insurance can reduce project risks and help make a project bankable, insurance premiums can be a substantial cost factor (especially for more exotic coverage). Therefore, the sponsor and its financial adviser must weigh the potential for increased financial market access and possibly lower interest rates against the premium costs on the insurance and consider the possibility of self-insurance.

3. Local Insurance/Reinsurance Issue. Many host countries require insurance for an international project to be issued by local companies. This raises issues of: the financial capacity of the local insurance market; the scope and nature of coverage available in the market; and the creditworthiness of the individual local insurer and its ability to pay proceeds in foreign currency. If there are constraints in the local market, one solution is for the local companies to reinsure most of their coverage with more creditworthy companies which are generally large international insurers. Reinsurance is an arrangement used by insurers to spread the risks that they assume when issuing policies. It is implemented through a reinsurance contract issued by the reinsuring party to the insurance company that originally issued the policy. This latter party is

called the primary insurer or ceding party. The primary insurer retains the direct underwriting relationship with the policy holder but is able to shift part of its liability under the original policy to a reinsurer by purchasing reinsurance.

Even if lenders are comfortable with the nature of the reinsurance arrangements, they still may not feel adequately protected. The reason is that any claim by the SPV must normally be made to the local company who is responsible for payment of the full amount of the coverage after collection from the reinsurers. If the local insurer has financial problems, difficulty in collecting from reinsurers and/or paying in foreign currency, the SPV (and its lenders) may not receive the full amount owing under the policy. To solve this problem, cut-through arrangements can be established which enable the SPV (and the lenders if they are co-insured) to bypass the local insurer and get direct payments from the reinsurers.

4. Insurance Provisions in Loan Agreements. Because of its great importance to lenders, loan agreements generally contain a number of provisions relating to insurance. Provisions may include: the right to approve the quality of the insurance companies and terms and conditions of policies; a requirement that the lenders be included in the loss payable clauses; a requirement that a notice of the assignment to the lenders of rights in the policy is endorsed on each policy; and the creation of cure rights for lenders in the event that the SPV does not pay the premium.

5.   Monoline Bond Insurance. Companies that provide insurance in connection with bond issues in the capital markets are known as monoline insurers. This type of insurance is sometimes referred to as a wrap guarantee and was first used extensively in the US municipal bond market to enhance access to the capital markets by US sub-sovereign entities. It has not gained widespread acceptance in international project financings but has been used in a few cases where monoline insurers or MDB's have given wrap guarantees to enhance bond issues in local currency for project financings. In the aftermath of the 2008/2009 financial crisis the future of the private sector monoline bond insurance market is uncertain, but MDB's and some bilateral agencies have continued to offer guarantees for bond issues.

C. Public Sector Support

One of the most important sources of third party credit support for private sector loans or equity investment in international projects is provided by various public sector entities, including the host government. Some host governments may be willing to provide various types of guarantees (e.g. guarantees of the input or offtake obligations of government owned entities) or subsidies (e.g. a subsidy of the capital cost of a project or subsidy of water or electricity tariffs for low income users). However, even in cases where a host government provides credit support for project debt, there may be a need for additional support from other public sector parties if the government is not deemed to be creditworthy or reliable. The main providers of this additional support are MDB's, ECA's and various specialized bilateral organizations. A variety of different credit support mechanisms are available from these institutions, and some of the more important programs are summarized in this section.

1.   Multilateral Development Banks. The MDB's as a group have several programs that provide varying degrees of support to private lenders and equity investors. The scope and details of the programs vary from institution to institution but they have enough in common so that the following generalizations are possible.

a.   *Guarantees: Partial Risk Guarantee.* A partial risk guarantee (PRG) is provided to lenders to protect them from loss resulting from SPV default on their loans caused by a government's failure to comply with specific undertakings the government had given to the SPV. The risks covered could include: convertibility and transferability of foreign exchange; breach of contract by a government or a government agency under a project agreement; a government breach of its obligation to pay compensation in the event of the termination of a concession; failure to provide needed permits or government approvals; changes in law or regulation; and interference with arbitration. The partial risk guarantee relates to the government's obligations and not the obligations of private party participants and is not a guarantee of debt service.

b.   *Guarantees: Partial Credit Guarantee.* The partial credit guarantee (PCG) is a guarantee of debt service and covers debt service payments against all risks irrespective of the cause of the default. The partial credit guarantee would cover defaults caused by the SPV, the contractor and other project participants as well as by the government and is not limited to breaches by government or government entities of government related risks. The partial credit guarantee is typically applied to the later maturities of a loan to extend the maturity on private sector loans to international projects.

c. *B–Loan Programs*. Under a B–Loan program, a MDB makes a two-tranche loan to the project entity. One tranche is called the A–Loan and is funded by the MDB out of its resources. The second tranche is called the B–Loan and is funded entirely by private sector lenders through participation agreements with the MDB. The private sector B–Loans loans are not guaranteed by the MDB but do share in the preferred creditor status of the MDB which would provide some comfort to the private lender. (For further details on B–Loan programs see the discussion in the section on preferred creditor status in Chapter 19).

d. *Political risk insurance*. Political risk insurance is provided by multilateral, bilateral and private sector institutions. The programs of the various providers vary considerably in scope of coverage, cost and maturity; but coverage is generally available in three broad areas: war and civil disturbance; expropriation; and currency inconvertibility and transfer. Some providers also cover breach of contract by governments. Other risks that are growing in importance for international projects and covered by some agencies include regulatory risk and sub-sovereign government risks.

The main source of multilateral political risk insurance is the Multilateral Investment Guarantee Agency (MIGA), a member of the World Bank Group. Its insurance provides a relatively broad coverage of political risks including: expropriation and creeping expropriation; adverse regulatory decisions and other adverse government or legislative action; governmental breach of contracts and nonpayment of arbitral awards related to such breaches; physical damage, business interruption or payment defaults caused by war, civil disturbance or terrorist activity; and currency convertibility and transfer.

e. *MDB Halo effect*. When an MDB participates in a project, it is said to create a halo-effect which may give some comfort to private sector lenders. This reflects the fact that the presence of a international agency may be an incentive for the other project participants (including the host government) to act more responsibly.

f. *Currency Devaluation Mitigation*. Some MDB's have attempted to develop programs that provide protection in cases where currency devaluation has an adverse impact on the project. For example, one method of providing this type of protection is through the creation of an MDB funded liquidity facility that would provide cash to the project in the event that a devaluation of local currency adversely affected hard currency debt repayment. To date, the efforts have been ad hoc and the institutions have not been able to mainstream these programs to provide any significant support for major international project financings.

2. Export Credit Agencies. Export credit agencies also offer commercial and political risk insurance, guarantee programs and interest equalization subsidies that facilitate private loans to international project financings. For example, when an ECA makes a direct loan to a project, it may also insure or guarantee a commercial bank loan for the same project; and this loan is referred to as a "covered loan." In addition, the presence of an ECA in a project financing provides some halo effect similar to that provided by the MDB's. It is hard to generalize further with respect to the ECA programs because there is great variation from country to country. For information on the programs of a specific ECA, the reader should check its website to see what types of credit support it offers for private sector loans to project financings.

3. Specialized Bilateral Agencies. A number of countries have specialized agencies that offer products that provide credit support in connection with international projects. A good example is the US Overseas Private Investment Corporation (OPIC) which is able to provide political risk insurance and guarantees to support both equity and debt for eligible international projects. Other countries also have agencies that provide various types of insurance, guarantees and foreign exchange mitigation products in support of private funding for international projects. See, for example, the websites of the 15 bilateral agencies that are members of the Association of European Development Finance Institutions (or EDFI).

D. Checklist of the Main Methods of Providing Credit Support for Project Loans

- Sound project economics
- Creditworthy and reliable project participants
- Appropriate risk allocation among project participants
- Quality and consistency of the basic project documents
- Strong sponsor support
  - Substantial equity contributions
  - Completion guarantees
  - Contingent equity for overrun funding
- Government support
  - Implementation agreements
  - Government backstop guarantees
  - Price subsidies
  - Shadow tolls and availability payments
- Contractual Credit Support
  - Fixed price, turnkey construction contracts
  - Strong off-take and supply agreements
  - Financial covenants in loan documentation
- Support through various types of guarantees
  - Completion guarantees
  - Financial guarantees

- Performance guarantees
- Specific risk guarantees
- Credit guarantees
- Letters of credit
- Bonding
- Multilateral Development Bank Support
  - Partial credit and partial risk guarantees
  - B–Loan programs
- Export Credit Agency Support
  - Insurance
  - Guarantees
- Bilateral Agency Support
  - Insurance
  - Guarantees
- Insurance
  - Commercial insurance covering construction and operational risks
  - Political risk insurance
- Security over project assets
- Direct agreements
- Payment trusts and other control accounts
- Hedging of risk through use of swaps and other derivative instruments

CHAPTER 14

SECURITY OVER PROJECT ASSETS

Previous chapters have considered how credit support for loans is provided to potential lenders through factors intrinsic to the project itself and various types of third party support. This section looks at two additional factors that provide protection and comfort to lenders: how assets of the project are used to provide collateral for loans to the project and the role of direct agreements in a project's security package.

A. Purpose of Security

There are several reasons why lenders generally insist on security over project assets. When a lender obtains a security interest, it normally obtains the right to possess and/or sell the collateral on the happening of certain specified events. In theory, the lenders could use this right to take control of the project assets and operate the project or sell them to help repay outstanding debt. For the lender to be able to do this effectively, the assets would need to be in good operating condition, have ascertainable value and be marketable without lengthy enforcement proceedings or government consents as a condition of use or sale. In addition, there are other more defensive reasons for taking security in project assets. They are:

- <u>Priority in Bankruptcy</u>: As secured creditors, lenders would have priority rights in liquidation or bankruptcy

- <u>Blocking Rights</u>: Lenders could prevent the SPV from selling the assets or prevent another creditor from acquiring security over the assets.

- <u>Negotiating Leverage</u>: The fact that lenders have the right to enforce their security interests is often useful as leverage when negotiating with the SPV.

B.   The Importance of Host Country Laws

The laws of the host country will generally govern all matters relating to the creation, perfection and enforcement of security in project assets. This means that a major issue for legal due diligence is the content of the host country laws relating to security. These laws will vary greatly from country to country and depend, in part, on whether the country has a civil or common law tradition. The basic question for due diligence is under what circumstances, and to what extent, the laws of the host country permit the seizure and sale of project assets or allow a creditor to take possession or ownership of project assets in order to operate the project.

C. Due Diligence Issues

To answer this general question, a number of subsidiary issues need to be considered, including:

1. <u>Assets Subject to Security Interests</u>. The threshold question is what types of assets are available for inclusion in the project's security package Specifically, is collateral limited to tangible fixed assets or may security interests be obtained in movable assets, intangible assets and future assets?

2. <u>Floating Charge Concept</u>. A floating charge "floats" over all of the borrowers' assets and fixes on those in possession when enforced. It enables ordinary business to be conducted before the floating charge fixes by allowing property to flow in and out of the possession of the debtor. A key question for due diligence is whether lenders can obtain a floating charge or whether its security interest has to be fixed on specific assets from the time that it is created.

3. <u>Process for Obtaining Security Interests</u>. Host countries will have different instruments, formalities and procedures for obtaining security interests. A part of due diligence is to understand exactly what needs to be done in the country concerned to perfect the interest. For example, does the lender need to take possession of an asset in order to perfect a security interest or are non-possessory security interests permitted? Is approval by the SPV and/or the host government needed to create a security interest? Are there special instruments or forms that need to be used? Are there special signing and notarial requirements? Are there limits on the amount of security? How should the document

be registered or recorded? What are the fees and the basis for calculating them?

4.   Assignment. Some countries may have restrictions on the assignment of security interests. For example, can the interest be assigned to a trust to be held by a trustee for the benefit of the lenders? In the case of syndicated bank loans, permitting such assignment would facilitate changes in the composition of the syndicate without the necessity of re-registering the security each time a bank is added or subtracted. When assigning a contract related to security interests is one also assigning performance obligations or the obligation for prior liabilities associated with the assets such as environmental pollution?

5.   Enforcement. There is great variation in how security interests are enforced from country to country. The lender due diligence process needs to determine exactly what needs to be done in the host country to convert the lender's security interest to ownership or control of assets that can used by the lenders or sold for cash to help repay outstanding loans. Security interests will be less valuable to lenders if the host country has lengthy, costly enforcement procedures where is outcome may be uncertain.

The great uncertainties that exist in many host countries in connection with the creation, perfection and enforcement of security interests diminish the importance of security over project assets in determining a project's bankability and the terms and conditions of its loans. This is one reason that lenders generally also insist on a pledge of the sponsor's shares in the SPV which may enable the lenders to exercise the rights of owners and not creditors and, in this way, escape the potential limitations inherent in the taking of security.

D. Direct Agreements

A direct agreement is a contract between the lenders, the SPV and a party to one of the project agreements, including the concession from the government. Direct agreements are related to the taking of security over project assets in that the two main purposes of entering into a direct agreement are: (1) to facilitate the ability of the lenders to take over a project by stepping into the shoes of the SPV/borrower if it defaults on its loan obligations and (2) to prevent the parties to the project agreements from terminating them without the consent of the lenders. To accomplish these objectives, clauses commonly found in direct agreements include:

- consent by parties to the project agreements (the "PA parties") to the creation of security in, or the assignment of, the SPV's rights under the project agreements;

- agreement by the PA parties that they will not terminate the project contract if lenders exercise their security rights;

- agreement by the PA parties not to exercise termination rights without giving notice to lenders;

- agreement by the PA parties that the lenders can assume the rights of the SPV under the contracts; and

- agreement by the PA parties and the government that all relevant licenses, consents and permits can be transferred to the lenders

The SPV, the PA parties and the government are generally willing to enter into direct agreements as they keep the lenders involved in trying to solve any problems with the project and may create obligations or limits on lender action. As an alternative to direct agreements, it may be possible to include provisions giving lenders rights in the various project documents and then rely on the contract law doctrine of third party beneficiary which is explicitly recognized by statute in some countries.

CHAPTER 15

OVERVIEW OF FINANCIAL DOCUMENTATION

This chapter begins consideration of the finance side documentation for a major international project. The final negotiation of the package of financial documents is one of the last stages of the long process of project preparation, and this chapter provides a very brief overview of its function and the documents that are included in it.

A. The Functions

The package of project documents is designed to help allocate risk, create the revenue stream and lay the foundation for a bankable project. The basic functions of the package of financial documents are to:

- set forth the mechanics and terms and conditions on which the loan is made, utilized and repaid;
- give lenders the right to refuse disbursement or require immediate repayment of outstanding loan principal in specified circumstances;
- provide lender control over the actions of the SPV;

- isolate and protect the revenue stream for the benefit of the lenders;
- provide credit support and security to ensure loan repayment; and
- establish rules governing relations among creditors.

The lenders receive approval from their loan committees or boards on the basis of assumptions as to how the project would be structured and carried out, and they are concerned that changes to the project might invalidate these assumptions and compromise loan repayment. The financial documents establish mechanisms that give the lenders the right to strictly control the actions of the SPV with respect to the project and to prevent any action that might jeopardize the maintenance of the revenue stream or divert it to other uses. In addition, they create events of default which act as early warning signals that something is wrong with the project and give lenders the right to cut their losses by suspending disbursements and declaring their loans immediately due and payable.

B.   Types of Financial Documentation

There is no standard package of financial documentation, and the specific documents used may vary from project to project depending on the nature of the transaction and the number and nature of the lending institutions involved. Some of the more common of these documents are listed and illustrated below.

Checklist of Financial Documents

Documentation Relating to Equity Funding

- equity subscription agreements
- sponsor overrun funding or contingent equity agreements
- provisions relating to equity contributions in the agreement among owners

Loan Agreement Documentation

- finance plan and financial model
- mandate letter appointing lead lenders
- preliminary term sheet
- offering memorandum
- the loan agreement(s)
    - commercial bank loan documentation
    - export credit loan documentation
    - multilateral development bank loan documentation
- common terms agreement
- B–Loan participation agreements
- capital market documentation
- sponsor subordinated debt
- closing documents and legal opinions

Loan Administration Documentation

- inter-creditor agreements
- agency and trustee agreements

- project account agreements
- collateral trust agreement

Credit Support and Security Documentation

- sponsor completion guarantee agreements
- other guarantee agreements
- share pledge agreements
- letters of credit
- bonding and surety documentation
- general insurance documentation
- security over project assets and concession rights
- documentation related to derivatives used in the transaction

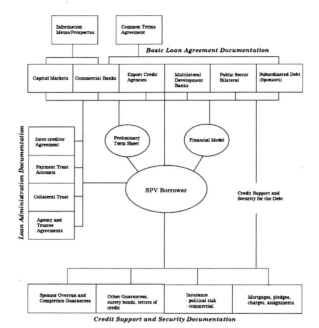

Credit Support and Security Documentation

DIAGRAM OF THE DEBT FINANCING DOCU-
MENTATION FOR AN INTERNATIONAL
PROJECT FINANCE TRANSACTION

CHAPTER 16

THE LOAN AGREEMENT

Loan agreements are the central documents in the package of agreements used to provide financial documentation and lender control over the SPV in international projects. The various categories of lenders will have different types of loan documentation based on their mandates and sources of funding; and individual lending institutions within these broad categories will have their own preferred version of a loan agreement. However, all of the agreements will have a large number of clauses in common. Commercial banks have been the main source of funding for international projects, and syndicated loans have been the main form of their lending. For this reason, the commercial bank syndicated loan agreement is used to illustrate a number of the basic concepts and clauses found in most loan documents.

A. Introduction to Syndicated Loans

Syndicated loans are transactions in which a group of banks (and often non-bank institutional lenders) join together to make a single loan to the borrower. Although there may be a large number of banks and non-bank institutions participating in the transaction, the loan is governed by a single, common loan agreement which is generally a very complex document. In order to provide background for the understanding of these agreements, this section of the chapter summarizes some of the key operational aspects of syndicated loan agreements

1. Function. The essence of any loan transaction is a promise to lend money and a promise to repay the money with interest at an agreed time or times in the future. The basic function of any loan agreement is to document the transaction by establishing the terms and conditions on which the loan is made, utilized and repaid and providing a description of the mechanics for disbursement and repayment. Syndicated loan agreements for international project finance are generally very lengthy documents because they also contain clauses designed to provide protection for lenders, control the actions of the SPV, provide for loan administration and deal with some intercreditor issues.

2. Types. There are different types of syndicated loans such as revolving facilities and term loans, and a syndicated loan is often divided into separate tranches or facilities which perform different functions by funding different stages or needs of the project. These tranches or facilities may have different drawdown procedures, maturities and repayment schedules which adds further complexity and complicates the drafting of multi-tranche syndicated loan agreements.

3. Funding. In order to understand some of the clauses in syndicated loan agreements, project finance lawyers should understand the assumptions

that are made as to how banks obtain the funds which they provide to the project. Many of the terms of the standard syndicated loan agreements are based on an assumption that the lending banks match-fund their loans to the project by taking deposits from other banks or financial institutions in the interbank market in amounts equal to their obligation to the borrower. The banks then relend the amount of the deposits to the project borrower. The interest rate that the bank charges on its loan to the SPV is based on the interest rate that the bank in theory had to pay in order to attract deposits. In the London market this rate is known as the London Interbank Offered Rate or LIBOR, and there are similar rates for the interbank markets in other major financial centers.

The interbank markets in which the banks are assumed to fund their loans are short term—with the most common maturities for deposits being 1, 3 or 6 months. Since syndicated loans for project financings are much longer term, each loan that a bank makes to the project is broken down into a series of short term interest periods which match the term of the deposits used to fund the loan. The interest charged in each period is based on the interbank market deposit rate for that period (plus a spread based on the lender's perception of risk). As a result, the interest rate the SPV pays changes every few months over the life of its match-funded loan and for this reason is said to be a "floating rate". These concepts underlie syndicated loan agreement clauses relating to determination of the rate of interest, the method and timing of requesting drawdowns, borrower options on interest payment dates and the various market disruption, margin protection and broken funding clauses discussed below.

4.　Process. At some stage in the process of arranging finance, the sponsors and their financial advisors will select the bank (often on the basis of competitive bidding) that they want to act as the lead bank in arranging a syndicated loan for the project. The sponsor and the lead bank also typically negotiate: (1) a Commitment Letter which, *inter alia*, confirms the appointment of the lead manager, sets forth the nature of its commitment to arrange the loan (i.e. fully underwritten or best efforts) and the fee arrangements; and (2) a Term Sheet which sets forth the general terms and conditions of the proposed loan and serves as the basis for the negotiation of the final loan agreement.

The lead bank and the borrower will also prepare an Offering or Information Memorandum to be used as part of the marketing effort to enlist a much larger group of banks to commit to lending as part of the syndicate. The commitment letter accompanying the term sheet may also contain provisions designed to enhance the prospects of success in marketing. The two most common are the clear market clause and the market flex clause. The clear market clause prohibits the sponsor from arranging or syndicating any other financing during a specified period while the financing for the project is being syndicated. The market flex clause gives lenders the flexibility to change pricing, structure and other terms in order to ensure a successful syndication in the face of deteriorating market conditions.

B. The General Structure of Loan Agreements

There is no standard loan agreement for international project financings, and complex international project financings often have several different types of lenders who would prefer to provide finance using their own form of loan documentation. Nonetheless, all lenders will have to deal with the same issues, and many use the same or similar clauses. There are different ways of categorizing the various issues and clauses found in loan agreements; and one useful way is to divide the clauses into broad groups according to the function that they perform as illustrated in the following checklist.

Basic terms of the loan

loan amount

interest rate

interest period

calculation of the interest rate

spread and fees

maturity

grace periods

amortization schedule

currency options

repayment options

prepayment

penalty interest

Mechanics of drawdown and repayment

conditions precedent to drawdown

minimum drawdown amounts

advance notice requirements

role of the agent bank

required legal opinions

repayment procedures

Lender protection and control over the actions of the borrower

conditions precedent to drawdown

representations and warranties

covenants

events of default

change of circumstances clauses

margin protection clauses

material adverse change clause

choice of law and forum for dispute settlement

maintenance of insurance obligations

reserved discretion clauses

Loan administration

agent bank

communications between SPV and the various lenders

loan repayment procedures

amendments and waivers

assignments of loans

Relations among lenders

role of the agent bank

pari passu or ratable treatment clause

voting majorities

Miscellaneous

definitions

special tax issues

dispute settlement

waiver of immunity clause

C. Key Clauses Commonly Found in Syndicated Loan Agreements

This section summarizes several of the key clauses that are commonly found in syndicated loan agreements. Some are unique to commercial bank loan documentation but the majority would also be found in the loan agreements of other types of lenders to international project financings. All of the summaries are highly simplified and intended to convey the general concept and not the nuances of the clauses.

1.   Categories of Lender Protection and Control Clauses. The sections on conditions precedent, representations and warranties and covenants are generally lengthy and contain long lists of items which

must be complied with by the borrower. Whether compliance is achieved is a decision made by the lenders in their subjective judgment which gives them great control over the SPV and the project. The precise items that are included in these general clauses would vary from project to project, but an example of the types of specific items covered is found in the table of contents of a typical common terms agreement found in Appendix 4.

a. *Conditions Precedent.* The purpose of the conditions precedent section is to list the various conditions that the borrower needs to satisfy before the lenders have an obligation to lend and the borrower can access funds under the loan agreement. The conditions are designed to provide lenders assurance that all the key contracts and other essential elements of the project are in place and that the project will be able to operate as expected. The conditions may relate to documents (e.g. the receipt of legal opinions) or performance (e.g. all required equity has been paid-in). Conditions precedent are generally divided into two categories: conditions precedent to the first drawdown and conditions precedent to subsequent drawdowns. For both the initial and subsequent drawdowns a lengthy set of conditions must be met; and for the subsequent draws some additional conditions may be required. In order to satisfy the conditions precedent to drawdown, the borrower must provide evidence satisfactory to the lender that they have all been met and legal opinions as to the validity and enforceability of the loan agreement and all other key documents relating to the project;

b. *Representations and Warranties.* The purpose of this category of clauses is to provide protection to the lenders by (1) assuring them that the project structure and assumptions that served as the basis for their credit decision continue to be true and (2) creating a basis for lenders to suspend disbursements or accelerate their loans by making breach of a representation or warranty an event of default under the loan agreement. The borrower is, in essence, saying to the lender that the facts set forth in a representation or warranty clause are true and that they will continue to be true in the future.

c. *Covenants.* The purpose of the covenant clause section is to provide assurance and protection to the lenders by obtaining various undertaking from the borrower relating to its future actions affecting the project. The covenants generally include agreement to: (1) take certain positive steps (e.g. affirmative covenants like provision of financial information and budgets and compliance with specified financial ratios) or (2) refrain from taking action that might impair the lender's interest in the project (e.g. negative covenants prohibiting the SPV from incurring additional debt, paying dividends unless financial ratios are met or creating security over project assets). In essence, the covenant sections help freeze the SPV borrower and the project structure in the condition that they were in when the lender first made the loan, ensure that no changes are made without lender consent, and provide assurance to the lenders that the project will be carried out efficiently and in accordance with sound industry practice.

d. *Events of Default.* The purpose of the events of default section is to establish a basis for the lenders to be able to suspend disbursements and accelerate their loans. The occurrence of some events of default give the lenders the right to accelerate immediately but most require that the lender provide notice to the borrower and give it a specified period of time to cure the default before the lenders' rights to exercise their remedies arise. The existence of an event of default also improves the lenders' bargaining position and may enable them to force a renegotiation in the event that they do not want to accelerate. Finally, when the borrower defaults—even if on a minor matter—it serves as an early warning system that there may be more fundamental problems with the project.

e. *Loan Acceleration.* Once an event of default has occurred, the acceleration clause provides lenders with the ability to (1) declare the amount of the loan that is outstanding to be immediately due and payable and/or (2) cancel any undrawn portion of the loan. This ability to accelerate loans is crucial for lenders in order to protect their interests in bankruptcy. Without this ability, the future loan repayments under the loan agreement would not constitute debt that was due and unpaid to serve as a basis for a priority claim in bankruptcy.

f. *Reserved Discretion.* The purpose of a reserved discretion clause is to give lenders the right to restrict the ability of the SPV to exercise rights under the various project agreements. The lenders want to be able to prevent any change in the project structure which might have a negative effect on the project's revenue stream and cash available for a debt service. Areas where lenders often reserve the right to make decisions (or to veto SPV decisions) with respect to the project agreements include: termination; issues relating to force majeure and insurance; SPV consent to a change order in the EPC contract; and the right to issue or approve a certificate of completion with respect to construction. Often the lenders are not satisfied with the protection and control afforded by a reserved discretion clause because of the lack of privity of contract with the other parties to the project agreements; and this may lead them to seek direct agreements with each party to key project agreements to obtain privity and greater control over the project.

g. *Right of Set–Off.* A set-off clause gives the lender the right to set-off (or reduce) any amount that it might owe to the borrower by the amount that the borrower owes to the lender under the loan agreement. For example, if the borrower had a deposit with a lending bank, that lender could reduce the amount of any deposit based liability it might have to the borrower by the outstanding amounts the borrower owed under the loan agreement. However, if the exercise of set-off rights enables a bank to receive amounts in excess of its pro rata share of principal and interest under the loan agreement, it might have to share this amount with the other banks in the syndicate under the sharing clause (See section on "Sharing of Payments" below).

2. Change of Circumstances Clauses. There are a number of clauses sometimes called change of circumstances clauses designed to provide protection to lenders when events occur which change the

underlying assumptions of the loan transaction. Two of the more important are:

a. *Illegality.* This clause is designed to deal with cases where it may have become illegal for a lender to continue to make the loan (e.g. lending to a particular country is prohibited for political reasons). If such illegality occurs, the lender is relieved of its obligation to continue to advance funds; and, if funds have already been advanced before the activity is made illegal, all the outstanding amounts become due and payable.

b. *Material Adverse Change.* The purpose of this clause is to protect lenders by enabling them to declare an event of default if the lenders believe that there has been a development that results in an adverse change in circumstances which has a material affect on the condition of the borrower or on its ability to comply with its obligations under the agreement. The lenders collectively decide whether there has been such an adverse change, but the decision must be reasonable and taken in good faith.

3. Margin Protection Clauses. Margin protection clauses deal with those changes in the assumptions prevailing at the time of the loan which affect the lender's spread or profit on the transaction. They are designed to ensure that the lenders suffer no financial loss as a result of the changes.

a. *Increased Cost.* The purpose of this clause is to pass on to the borrower any increased costs that a lender might experience due to changes in law or regulatory requirements (e.g. an increase in reserve requirements or tax in the lender's home country).

In the event that the costs to the lender of making a loan increase due to regulatory changes, the lender's profit would be reduced; and the increased cost clause requires the borrower to pay the increased costs to maintain the lender's profit margin.

b.   *Capital Cost.* Similarly, if the amount of capital that a lender has to hold against its loan commitments is increased by law or by regulatory action, the effective cost of lending would be increased and the lender's rate of return would be reduced. As in the case of the illegality clause, the borrower would be required to cover the increased costs.

c.   *Tax Gross-up.* The purpose of this clause is similar to the increased cost clause in that it shifts risk to the borrower when a withholding tax is imposed by the borrower's country. If such a tax is imposed, the clause requires the borrower to assume the tax and pay an additional amount to the lender so that it receives the amount that it would have received if there had been no withholding tax In this way the borrower makes a gross-up payment to the lender.

d.   *Market Disruption or Eurodollar Disaster.* The purpose of this clause is to deal with cases where there has been a general disruption in the financial markets which means that banks cannot obtain funds in the interbank market to match fund their loans to the borrower or LIBOR does not adequately reflect the cost to the banks of funding their loans. If either of these circumstances exist, the clause requires the parties to negotiate an alternative interest rate basis for the loan.

e. *Broken Funding*. The purpose of this clause is to compensate lenders for any costs it may incur if the borrower prepays or fails to drawdown after it has filed a drawdown request. Since it is assumed that lenders match-fund their loans for each interest period in the interbank market, any prepayment or failure to drawdown may cause the lender to incur costs by paying interest on its borrowing in the interbank market that is not recovered through interest it receives on its loans to the project. The broken funding clause is intended to indemnify lenders for these costs.

4. Clauses Dealing With Relations Among the Lenders. A syndicated loan agreement will have a series of clauses dealing with relations among the banks participating in the loan and with other lenders to the same borrower.

a. *Cross Default*. The purpose of this clause is to ensure that creditors who lend to a borrower under one loan agreement (Agreement A) will be in a position to enforce their rights against the borrower in cases where a different set of creditors under a different loan agreement (Agreement B) become entitled to enforce their rights against the borrower. If a default occurs under Agreement B and the lenders under that agreement become entitled to accelerate their loan, this event automatically becomes an event of default under Agreement A even though there has been no other default under Agreement A. This means that the creditors under Agreement A will have the right to take action against the borrow or its assets at the same time as the creditors under Agreement B.

b. *Pari–Passu*. The purpose of this clause is twofold: (1) to ensure equality of treatment among all members of the syndicate and (2) to ensure that the borrower does not have (or will not create) a class of creditors whose claims rank senior to the debt which is the subject of the agreement in which the clause is found. This is accomplished by inserting *pari passu* language in both the "representations and warranties" section and in the "covenants" section of the agreement. In the former section, the borrower represents that the debt covered by the agreement ranks *pari passu* with all of the borrower's non-subordinated debt and that it has no secured debt outstanding other than that which has disclosed to the lenders. In the latter section, the borrower agrees that it will maintain this equality in the future.

c. *Negative Pledge*. The purpose of this clause is to ensure that all of a borrower's assets are free from encumbrances and available to satisfy the claims of all unsecured creditors in times of financial distress. The clause accomplishes this result by (1) creating an absolute prohibition on incurring any future secured debt without the consent of the existing lenders or (2) permitting additional secured debt only if the party that would otherwise be protected by the clause is "equally and ratably secured". In short, the clause is a restriction on the ability of the borrower to grant preferential security interests to subsequent creditors

d. *Sharing of Payments*. This clause is designed to prevent a borrower from discriminating in favor of a certain lender or group or lenders when it makes payments to members of a loan syndicate. It would come into play if one member of a syndicate receives more than it was entitled to under the loan agreement. The clause is a covenant among the lenders and not an agreement between the borrowers and the lenders; and equitable sharing can be achieved by turning the excess over to the agent who redistributes it proportionately.

5.   Dispute Resolution Clauses. Loan agreements will also have clauses dealing with dispute resolution which include (a) a governing law clause whose purpose is to designate the law to be used in interpreting the agreement; (b) a submission to jurisdiction clause in which the lenders choose the forum—usually New York or England—in which they want to enforce the agreements even though courts in that forum may not have personal jurisdiction over the borrower; and (c) a waiver of immunity clause in which a governmental party waives its claim to sovereign immunity to ensure lenders that it will not be able to avoid suit by imposing an immunity defense.

D.   Ancillary Documents

There are a number of other financial documents that are closely related to, or integrated with, loan agreements. Three of the most common are:

1.   Common Terms Agreement. The fact that there is no standard loan documentation creates a coordination problem when there are several lenders each proposing to use their own loan agreements which may have differing terms and conditions. In such cases, an effort will be made to

minimize intercreditor issues by creating a common terms agreement (sometimes called a common agreement). This agreement would contain terms and conditions agreed by all the lenders and applicable to all loans for the project in such areas as drawdown mechanisms, conditions precedent to drawdowns, representations and warranties, covenants and events of default. Any terms and conditions specific to individual lenders would be included in separate loan agreements that each lender would negotiate with the borrower. (A table of contents of a typical common terms agreement used in international project financings is provided in Appendix 4 as an example of the scope of this document)

2. Closing Memorandum. Even after the parties have reached final agreement on the terms and conditions of the loan agreement, the lenders have no legal obligation to lend until the agreement has been signed, declared to be effective and the conditions precedent for loan disbursement have been met by the borrower. These actions are typically taken as what is known as the closing. The closing proceedings are documented in a Closing Memorandum which serves as a checklist and organizing document describing all of the documents, parties and transactions required for the completion of the closing. If properly done, the Closing Memorandum can also serve as a type of historical narrative of the transaction.

3. Legal Opinions. An essential aspect of every closing is the delivery of legal opinions to provide assurance to lenders that the legal basis of the transaction is sound and that the legal assumptions

on which the lenders approved their loans are still valid at the time of the closing and/or drawdown of the funds. The lenders will expect to receive opinions with respect to the loan agreement and all other documents critical to the success of the project as well as any other material legal issues that may be unique to the specific project. The opinions are a way of providing added comfort to lenders as they know that the law firm is putting its reputation on the line when it signs and delivers its opinion and that, in order to give the opinion, its lawyers will undertake final due diligence to make sure that there have been no last minute adverse developments.

CHAPTER 17

LOAN ADMINISTRATION AND PROJECT ACCOUNTS

A number of administrative functions need to be performed in connection with loans for major international project financings. These functions include (1) communication among, and collective decision making by, the various lenders to the project and (2) management of project cash flow and security over project assets. While some of these issues will be dealt with in the basic loan agreements, more detailed separate agreements may also be needed in complex project financings. The most common of these agreements are: a Collateral Agency Agreement; a Project Account Agreement; and an Intercreditor Agreement.

A. Syndicated Loan Administration

Syndicated loan agreements will have provisions appointing an agent bank to administer the loan and setting forth its duties. The agent bank acts for all of the lenders in the syndicate and is the main channel of communication among the banks and between the borrower and the participating banks. It may also calculate interest and principal payments, monitor compliance with covenants in the

165

loan agreement and serve as a channel for disbursement and receipt of payments of debt service by the borrower. It is also a party, on behalf of the syndicate of banks, to the various other administrative agreements noted above. In performing its functions, the agent bank generally has no discretion unless specifically provided.

B. Collateral Agency Agreement

A trust is often created to hold collateral and security over project assets for the benefit of the lenders. The Collateral Agency Agreement would appoint a collateral agent who would be given the powers to: accept, administer, preserve and protect the security; appoint a separate trustee to hold the security if necessary; execute security documents on behalf of the lenders; register and perfect the security interests; and enforce and foreclose on security.

C. Project Account Agreement

Every major project finance transaction will have a system of project accounts that are used to collect, manage and allocate the cash flow generated by loan proceeds and the project's revenue stream. Accounts are used in both the construction and operating phases for a variety of purposes and include both off-shore accounts and accounts in the host country. Account structure is tailored to the needs of the individual project so there is substantial variation from project to project.

1. <u>Purpose</u>. The basic purpose is to control and monitor the cash flow and establish reserves to be used in the event the revenue stream is interrupted or diminished. The accounts would be established pursuant to a Project Account Agreement which would (1) appoint an agent to administer the agreement; (2) establish an overall account structure with various accounts (and sub-accounts) and mechanisms for the deposit and application of loan proceeds and the project revenue stream; and (3) prioritize the way in which the cash flow would be allocated to various categories of project expenses, reserves and distributions. A simplified summary of a possible structure of operational period accounts for a major international project financing is provided in the following paragraphs.

2. <u>Operational Period Accounts</u>. There is a primary general account that serves as a holding account for the revenue stream that is created by the payments from the off-takers or users of the project. In addition, there are a number of "sub-accounts" that are used to accumulate funds for specific project related purposes. Lenders to international projects prefer to have the primary account and as many other accounts as possible located outside the host country to minimize potential problems with currency convertibility or transfer and other host country control over the funds.

a. *Primary Account*. The funds that are paid into the primary account are then allocated to the sub-accounts and used to pay the operating, debt service and other expenses before making any dividend or other distributions to the SPV shareholders. The agreement establishing the account will establish the priority in which the various payments should be made. A typical prioritization of expenditures might be as follows:

Category I: Costs necessary to keep the project in operation to continue generation of the revenue stream. These costs would include all essential operating costs including, fuel, raw materials and other inputs;

Category II: Taxes;

Category III: Payments of interest on debt, payments pursuant to interest rate swap transactions, agency fees, and any other payments necessary to stay current on debt obligations;

Category IV: Repayment of principal on debt obligations and termination payments under swap transactions;

Category V: Payments to any special reserve accounts established in connection with the project to ensure that the project will always have some cash available in the event the expected revenue and cash flow stream is interrupted or diminished. (e.g. debt service reserve account; major maintenance account; or a standard operating and maintenance account);

Category VI: Prepayment of debt under a "cash sweep" provision that provides that all or a portion of any cash left in the account after satisfying other obligations should be used to prepay debt to reduce it maturity; and

Category VII: Dividends or other distributions to the shareholders of the SPV.

Under this system of prioritization, the funds that flow into the primary account are allocated to the sub-accounts in such a way that the funds are used to pay the items in the various categories on a "cascade" or "waterfall" basis. This means that any available funds would first be used to pay Category I costs with any remaining funds then flowing down to pay Category II expenditures, then Category III expenditures and so on until there were no more funds available.

b. *Sub-accounts.* The sub-accounts that are often created to accumulate project receipts and cash flow to be held until needed for payment or other specific purposes include:

Operating Cost Account

Tax Payment Account

Debt Service Payment Account

Various Reserve Accounts

Shareholder Distribution Account

See the following diagram for an example of a "waterfall" system.

c. *Other Accounts.* In addition to the general primary account and its various sub-accounts which receive and allocate the cash generated by the project's revenue stream, there are often accounts established to receive, hold and allocate funds received from other sources. These accounts are often called Compensation or Proceeds Accounts as the sources of the funds are generally proceeds from insurance received after damage to the project facilities, liquidated damages received under the provisions of one of the project agreements or the proceeds from successful litigation or arbitral claims. The funds received would be held and then used to repair or replace project facilities, pay down project debt in the case of performance liquidated damages or supplement cash flow from the revenue stream.

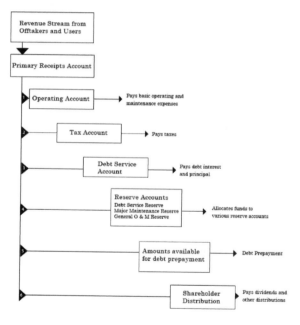

SIMPLIFIED DIAGRAM OF OPERATIONAL
PERIOD "WATERFALL" ACCOUNTS

CHAPTER 18

USE OF DERIVATIVES IN INTERNA-TIONAL PROJECT FINANCING

Most major international project financings involve the use of derivative transactions to mitigate financial and commodity risk. In fact, project finance loan agreements often contain covenants requiring the SPV to enter into and maintain specified hedging transactions. The material in this section is intended to provide a brief introduction to the use of derivatives in international project financing

A. General Considerations

1. <u>What Are Derivatives?</u> Derivatives are financial instruments that derive their value from some other more basic instrument, asset, or variable which is referred to as the "underlier". Underliers include: commodity prices, interest rates, a currency, a stock price, a bond price, a stock exchange index, or other financial index or instrument. When the value of the underlier changes, the value of the derivative instrument will also change.

2. <u>Basic Forms of Derivative Instruments</u>. There are four basic types of derivatives which are commonly used as building blocks to create more complex derivative instruments. They are:

- *forward contracts* which are agreements to buy or sell a specific amount or value of an underlier at a specified future date at a specified price;

- *futures contracts* which are standardized, publicly traded forward contracts that are executed on organized exchanges;

- *option contracts* which require the payment of an option premium fee and which grant the holder a right, but not the obligation, to buy (or sell) a specific amount of the underlier on or before a specified date for a specified price; and

- *swap contracts* which are agreements in which the counterparties agree to exchange future cash flows by making periodic payments to each other for a specified period.

3. Main Uses of Derivative Contracts. Some basic derivative instruments have been used for decades to hedge risk inherent in business and financial transactions. Hedging is generally defined as engaging in a transaction that offsets (either fully or partially) the risks associated with another event or transaction. Agricultural commodity price risk has been hedged in the U.S. since the mid–1800's and in more recent decades derivatives have been used to mitigate interest rate and currency risk and equity and credit market risks. In addition to hedging adverse changes in the value of a company's liabilities or assets, derivatives are used to speculate by assuming risk in an attempt to profit from anticipated changes in the value of the underlier. They are also used to obtain more desirable terms for commercial bank and capital market borrow-

ings, to change the asset mix of portfolios of securities and to offset credit exposure risks.

4.   Documentation of Derivative Transactions. The International Swaps and Derivatives Association, Inc. (ISDA), has created a set of standardized documents to govern derivatives transactions in an effort to simplify documentation and provide certainty, uniformity and efficiency in the market. The basic package of documents includes:

- a standard document known as the ISDA Master Agreement which enables two derivative counterparties to have a single agreement governing transactions that they conduct with each other. The theory is that each individual transaction between the parties is entered into on the basis of the terms and conditions of the Master Agreement and that all individual transactions are combined with the Master Agreement to form a single agreement. The ISDA Master Agreement is a pre-printed agreement that deals with basic issues such as netting and other payment mechanics, standard representations and warranties, events of default creating termination rights, and procedures for termination and calculation of termination values;

- a Schedule to the ISDA Master Agreement which gives the parties the opportunity to modify and supplement the Master Agreement in order to address issues specific to the parties and the transaction and to set forth any special conditions precedent to the transaction;

- a Credit Support Annex for use in the event the parties are required to provide collateral in connection with their obligations;

- a confirmation that sets forth the specific economic and financial terms of each individual transaction; and

- a set of documents containing standard definitions that can be referenced by the parties in conducting and documenting their transactions.

B. Use of Derivatives in International Project Financings

1. <u>Mitigation of Specific Project Risks</u>. The main uses of derivative transactions in an international project financing are to hedge interest rate, currency and commodity price risks. Interest rate swaps are the most common derivative used in international project financings. They, in essence, convert an SPV's floating rate interest obligations into fixed rate interest obligations in order to eliminate risk to the project's cash flow from large swings in floating rate interest rates on outstanding loan balances. Likewise currency swaps are sometimes used to convert the SPV's debt repayment and other foreign currency obligations from one currency to another. An international project financing is often subject to the risks of commodity price fluctuations, and these risks are often hedged by using forward or futures contracts. Examples of the use of derivatives in project financing include: a coal fired power project that uses forward contracts to hedge risk for

both the price at which it sells electricity and the purchase price of coal and other input costs; a gold mining project that uses derivatives to hedge against the risk of a fall in gold prices; and a contractor that uses the forward markets to hedge against possible foreign exchange losses in connection with the purchase of major equipment that might result from currency movements between the time the purchase contract was signed and the time of delivery.

2.   Loan Agreement Provisions Dealing With Derivatives. Many loan agreements will contain provisions relating to the use of derivatives in connection with the project. These provisions may include: a specific requirement that the SPV use derivative transactions to protect against specified project risks; requirements as to the quality and creditworthiness of the SPV's counterparties; restrictions on the provision of collateral to derivative providers; lender cure rights; and protection against loss in the event that a provider of derivatives to the SPV defaults. The lender due diligence process needs to compare the provisions of the loan agreement and the swap documentation to ensure that there are no mismatches in their terms.

3.   Limits on the Use of Derivatives in International Project Financings. While the use of derivatives can be an effective way to hedge against project risks, there are some limits on their use in international project financings. For infrastructure projects that earn only local currency, it may be difficult to enter into currency swaps between a host country's local currency and the currency of debt repayment as the markets for this type of local

currency/international currency swap are often limited and/or very expensive. In addition, concerns about the creditworthiness of the SPV or the project may make derivative transactions impractical because other parties to the transaction may not be willing to accept the SPV as a counterparty without excessive collateral or compensation.

4. Added Risks Involved in the Use of Derivatives. While derivative transactions may help mitigate certain types of project risks, they can also add new risks which need to be monitored. For example, interest rate and currency swaps involve the swapping of future payment streams; and each party to the swap is exposed to a counterparty risk in that the other party may not make timely payment on its obligations. To protect against this risk, one or both of the parties may be required to post collateral; and the SPV's counterparty may claim that it should become a secured party under the project's existing security arrangements and have voting rights under the Intercreditor Agreement. In addition, if for some reason, the swap needs to be terminated and unwound, there will be termination payments and other costs to one or both of the parties that are known as "a breakage" costs that will need to be paid. The need to deal with these risks may further complicate intercreditor relations.

C. Intercreditor Issues Raised by Hedge Provider Involvement

When hedge providers and hedging contracts are involved in the project, a number of intercreditor issues are raised. In many cases the providers of the hedging transactions are also lenders to the SPV which raises issues concerning their relationship to the other lenders to the transaction. The specific issues will vary with the project and the nature of the hedging transaction, but common matters that need to be considered by the lawyers for both the lenders and the hedge providers include:

- Does the hedge provider need to be a party to any of the basic financing documents and, if so, should it have voting rights? Should the lenders have the right to restrict actions by the hedge providers by requiring prior consent of the lenders before certain specified actions can be taken?

- What priority should be established (1) as between the ongoing payments under the hedge contracts and the payment of interest on the loans and (2) as between any lump sum termination payments under the hedge contracts and principal payments under the loan agreements? Should the hedge providers participate in the project's cash waterfall? If so, on what basis (e.g. ongoing, ordinary course payments under the hedge contracts included in the interest payment pool)?

- Should hedge providers be permitted to have a security interest in project assets as collateral? If so, how should collateral under the hedge contracts and the loan contracts and related collateral agreement be shared? Should hedge providers have a voice in determining when project collateral is enforced?

- Should all project debt obligations including obligations under hedge contracts be accelerated at the same time or, at least, subject to cross-default that would trigger simultaneous or cross-acceleration? How, in general, should acceleration be coordinated?

- How should lenders deal with the fact that in some countries derivative transactions may have favored treatment in bankruptcy proceedings?

CHAPTER 19

INTERCREDITOR ISSUES

Issues among creditors in international project financings arise most frequently when there are different types of lenders—multilateral development banks, export credit agencies, private commercial banks and bond investors—involved in the same project. This section discusses some of the most common intercreditor issues.

A. Overview

The need for documentation to govern relations among creditors in an international project financing arises at two levels. The first is at the syndicate level to deal with the relationships among the banks participating in a syndicated commercial bank loan, and the second deals with the relationships among the different types of lenders or credit support providers to the same project. The relations among the banks within a commercial bank syndicate are generally governed by the provisions of the loan agreement, and industry practice in this area has become relatively standardized and the legal issues that need to be dealt with are relatively routine. The relationships among the different categories of lenders in an international project financing are dealt with in an Intercreditor Agreement and generally raise more difficult legal issues.

B. Intercreditor Agreement

In a major international project financing the parties to the Intercreditor Agreement could include:

- the Intercreditor Agent
- the SPV/Project Company
- the sponsors/shareholders of the SPV (as subordinated lenders)
- international and local commercial banks (through their agent banks)
- multilateral development institutions as lenders and/or guarantors
- export credit agencies as lenders and/or guarantors
- the collateral agent or trustee
- bond issue trustees
- hedging counterparties

The basic provisions in most Intercreditor Agreements include: (1) the appointment of an Intercreditor Agent; (2) clauses providing for *pari passu* treatment of all creditors and for pro rata sharing of the proceeds from the enforcement of security and any other proceeds that one of the lenders might receive; and (3) decision making and voting arrangements for amendment of agreements, the grant of waivers, the enforcement of security, and acceleration of loans.

Difficult negotiations arise in projects where one or more of the creditors assert that certain payments to them should be excluded from the operation of the *pari passu* and pro rata sharing provisions of the Intercreditor Agreement. For example, MDB's often want to treat any payments that they receive as preferred creditors as "excluded payments" under the agreement.

Negotiation of voting rights also can be difficult when the lender group includes both private sector lenders such as commercial bank syndicates or bond purchasers and public sector lenders like MDB's and ECA's. Issues that may arise in connection with voting include: whether the capital markets tranche, guarantors and hedge providers should have voting rights; how voting rights should be calculated and allocated; the percentage vote needed to enable remedies to be taken and loans to be accelerated; and whether one creditor or creditor group will have veto power over specific actions that other institutions might wish to take.

C. Specific Intercreditor Issues

The presence of multilateral development banks and political risk insurers creates some unique problems that are discussed in this section.

1. Preferred Creditor Status: In General

a. *Basic Concept.* The two key elements of preferred creditor status are: (1) certain creditors are accorded preferential treatment by their borrowers in the allocation and/or transfer of foreign exchange in cases where the country has imposed exchange controls or where there is insufficient foreign exchange to repay all external debts and (2) the loans of lenders enjoying preferred creditor status are generally not subject to debt rescheduling.

b. *Categories of Preferred Creditors.* The main categories of lenders traditionally afforded preferred creditor status are: the multilateral financial institutions; short term trade and supplier creditors; and bondholders. In addition, commercial banks and institutional investors share some of the preferred status of a multilateral development bank when they participate in the various B–Loan programs of the MDB's as described below. In the project finance context, the multilateral development banks are the category of lenders that most frequently claim preferred creditor status.

c. *Applications and Consequences.* When a multilateral development bank is involved in an international project financing, preferred creditor issues sometimes arise between the MDB and the other lenders, especially export credit agencies and occasionally other MDB's who also expect preferred creditor treatment. It arises because the other lenders are treated as subordinated lenders as a result of MDB refusal to accept the standard *pari passu* and sharing clauses in loan documentation and inter-creditor agreements. Since most export credit agencies and MDB's have policies against taking a subordinated position, discussions take place between the different categories of public sector lenders involved, and some compromise is generally reached.

2.   Preferred Creditor Status: B–Loan Transactions

a.   *Concept.* B–Loan transactions are loans where a MDB shares some of its preferred creditor status with private sector commercial banks and sometimes institutional investors. The B–Loan transaction involves two principal documents:

- one loan agreement between the MDB and the borrower covering two tranches: an A Loan using the MDB's own funds and a B–Loan using funds provided by the private sector lenders who purchase participations in the B–Loan tranche. The funding for 100% of the amount of B–Loan is provided by the private sector lenders; and

- a Participation agreement between the MDB and each bank or institutional investor.

The MDB is the sole lender of record as far as the borrower is concerned and acts as administrator of both the A and B loan tranches. The fact that it is lender of record for both tranches means that it is able to share its preferred creditor status with the private sector lenders.

b.   *The Benefits.* There are several benefits to the private sector participants which help mitigate risks and induce them to lend to a project that they might not otherwise find bankable. There are some minor differences in the B–Loan programs of the various MDB's, but the private participants generally enjoy the following benefits:

- although the private sector B-loans are not guaranteed by the MDB, they share in the MDB's preferred creditor status which gives the MDB a preferred allocation of foreign exchange;

- the MDB shares any funds it receives in repayment of the loan with the B–Loan participants on a pro rata basis;

- they benefit from the "halo" or "umbrella" effect of the presence of an MDB in the transaction as a borrower may be less likely to default since its loan is from an MDB;

- the private sector participants are exempt from any withholding tax in the borrowing country and may be exempt from various regulatory requirements imposed by their home governments, including reserve requirements and mandatory loan loss provisioning;

- for internal credit risk and capital adequacy purposes, the participation may count as a loan to an AAA borrower rather than a lesser rated, emerging market borrower; and

- rating agencies may consider a B–Loan as a way to mitigate country risk and will take this into account in granting ratings for loans to the project.

The main benefit to the MDB from sharing its preferred creditor status is that can make a smaller loan to the project and preserve some of its lending authority to fund additional projects.

3. Negative Pledge Clause

a. *The Concept.* The negative pledge clause (or "NPC") is a common loan agreement covenant found in the loan agreements of both public sector lenders like the multilateral development banks and private sector commercial banks. There are different formulations of the precise language of the clause. Some clauses contain an absolute prohibition on new liens, and others permit liens but require that the unsecured lenders be equally and ratably secured by giving them the same security as the new secured lenders. Despite the different approaches, in all cases the NPC restricts a borrower's ability to create liens on its assets in order to grant a priority to certain creditors.

The major multilateral development banks generally lend to governments and other public sector borrowers on an unsecured basis and have NPC's in their public sector loan agreements. These clauses effectively prevent the creation of any new lien on a country's governmental assets unless a waiver is given by the MDB. Most MDB clauses apply only to "public assets" and "external debt" and are concerned only with protecting priority for their loans in the allocation, realization or distribution of foreign exchange.

b. *The Application in International Project Financing.* MDB negative pledge clauses seldom create a problem for most international project financings because project assets are owned by the SPV and are not public assets. Only in the rare case where the SPV is controlled by a state owned entity would the assets be considered governmental assets. In such a case, the MDB negative pledge clause would prevent another lender from taking security in the SPV's assets unless a waiver was granted. This would be the case even if the MDB was not a lender to the project in question because of the presence of negative pledge clauses in the other loan agreements the MDB has with the government. In contrast with the MDB's, it is not unusual for commercial bank loan agreements to have an exception to their NPC covenants for project financings and permit liens on assets which are the subject of the project financing or revenues which arise from the operation of such assets.

4.   Concern with Offshore Escrow Accounts. Various multilateral institutions and some governments have, from time to time, expressed concern over the use of the use of offshore escrow accounts to receive and hold foreign exchange earned through the exports from an international project financing. Even though they recognize the fact that such accounts may actually create opportunities for lenders to support projects that would make a net positive contribution to a country's foreign exchange earnings, they still generally oppose their use. The basic reason is that they consider the trust a pledge of future revenues which provides preferential treatment to certain creditors and reduces a country's flexibility to manage its foreign exchange reserves. In short, they believe that the use of an offshore trust creates a preference over the foreign exchange assets of the host country which would

have the effect of subordinating all other loans that do not share in the account and possibly threatening the preferred creditor status of multilateral lending institutions.

5. <u>Conflicting Interests in the Pledged Shares of the SPV</u>. The political risk insurers of equity investors in the SPV and the lenders to the SPV often have conflicting interests in the event that SPV assets are expropriated and the insurers pay compensation to the shareholders of the SPV. The conflict arises because of the conflicting claims on the shares of the SPV by the lenders and the insurer. If the insurer pays compensation, it becomes subrogated to the rights that the insured party had against the host government and obtains a right to assert the same claim for compensation against the host government that the insured SPV shareholder had. As a condition of paying compensation, the insurer generally requires the insured equity investor to deliver its shares in the SPV to the insurer free and clear of any liens or other encumbrances. On the other hand, the lenders would generally require a pledge of the same shares held by the SPV shareholders as part of the collateral package for their loans. Thus, there is a direct conflict between the insurer and the lenders over who has the priority claim on SPV shares. There is no easy solution to this dilemma which often results in difficult negotiations between insurers and lenders.

PART V

WHEN PROBLEMS ARISE

CHAPTER 20

RENEGOTIATION AND RESTRUCTURING

The renegotiation of financial and investment transactions is common in international business. This is especially true in the international project finance field as most projects are long-term undertakings that involve a set of business, financial and political factors that change over time. As a result, the project finance community has accepted the fact that even the most carefully structured projects may need to be renegotiated or restructured.

A. Renegotiation Clauses

A well designed contract will include provisions to allow the parties to readjust their relationship. The types of renegotiation or adaptation clauses vary from agreement to agreement depending on the parties, the nature of the project and the applicable governing law. The most common are:

1. <u>Automatic Review Clauses</u> where the parties agree to meet periodically to review whether the

contract continues to operate fairly and to try to
negotiate solutions to any problems that arise;

2.   Automatic Adjustment Clauses where tariffs
and other key financial and economic factors are
automatically adjusted pursuant to a relevant index
or other indicator such as inflation, currency movements or input costs; and

3.   Specific Renegotiation Clauses which can be
of two types: those that identify specific events that
would result in renegotiation and general clauses
that do not refer to specific events but which would
require negotiations in cases of economic hardship
or distortion in the economic equilibrium of the
contract.

If a contract does not establish the details of the
procedures for renegotiation, guidelines provided by
case law and commentators suggest that the talks
should be carried out in good faith in search for an
acceptable compromise, last for a period that is
appropriate under the circumstances and demon-
strate awareness of the interests of the other party.

B.   Elements of a Restructuring

1.   Process. There are three commonly recognized phases in the restructuring process for an
international project financing: the conflict and confrontation stage; the standstill phase; and a final
phase in which new arrangements and relationships
are agreed and implemented. In the conflict and
confrontation stage, the parties begin to realize that
there are serious problems with the project and
often take actions that escalate the difficulties such

as threats to cancel contracts or institute litigation. In most (but not all) cases, the parties soon realize that it is in everyone's best long run interest to try to reach a negotiated rather than a litigated solution. As a result, they agree on a standstill period during which all parties agree to refrain from pursuing remedies while trying to negotiate a more permanent solution. During this stage, they will undertake a assessment of what went wrong and conduct an extensive new due diligence exercise with respect to both project and financial documents. The results of this due diligence will serve as the basis for new long term agreements that embody the terms of the renegotiated and restructured project

2. <u>Elements of a Standstill Agreement</u>. The basic concept of the standstill is to provide the project participants with some time to cool-off from the initial conflict and to try to work out a coordinated solution. Under a standstill agreement, there is a temporary waiver of existing defaults and agreement by all parties to refrain from taking any legal action or exercising other remedies. In addition, the agreement would provide for either a debt service moratorium or the continuation of some payments on a substantially reduced basis to show good faith by the borrower. There may also be some reduction in the tariff or prices paid by offtakers if consumer resistance is one of the elements that created the need to renegotiate. Standstill agreements are generally short term (e.g. six months) in order to keep the pressure on all parties to reach a solution but they are customarily extended if there is evidence of progress.

3.   Institutional and Organizational Aspects. In the case of restructuring of syndicated bank loans for a traditional corporate or sovereign financing, a formal Bank Steering Committee composed of representatives of the major syndicate participants is generally created. While this committee does not have the power to bind the rest of the lenders in the syndicate, it provides an organized focal point for the negotiations and a channel of communication among the participants and between the syndicate and the borrower. In the case of the renegotiation and restructuring of an international project financing, the process is less formal and more ad hoc in nature as a more diverse group of creditors is generally involved. (e.g. ECA's, MDB's, political risk insurers, and bilateral agencies as well as commercial banks and possibly bondholders).

4.   Prerequisites to a Successful Restructuring. The issues that need to be considered in order to fully understand what went wrong and the various steps that need to be taken to resolve the problems on a sustainable basis include:

- an assessment of the basic causes of the need for restructuring;

- an updating of market conditions and long run demand forecasts;

- a revised financial analysis based on projections of future cash flow to determine a new sustainable level of debt and debt service payments;

- review of all project and finance documents to determine how a restructuring might affect obligations under the contracts;

- identification of the consents, approvals and waivers needed from each lender and each party to a project agreement;

- review of the security arrangements for the project and determination of what (if any) changes need to be made;

- review all covenants in the loan agreement to see which are affected and what notice needs to be given to lenders; and

- an evaluation of creditor voting requirements needed to approve the restructuring.

5.   Variables in a Debt Restructuring. The new terms and conditions for the debt must be payable under an affordable, sustainable and politically acceptable tariff which is tailored to the available cash flow and provides for debt service obligations that are sustainable over the remaining life of the loan. The variables which may need to be adjusted to meet these conditions include: interest rates; grace periods; amortization schedules; maturities; principal reduction via haircut, write-off or debt-equity swap; and pricing of project output or services.

6.   Political and Social Dimensions. In addition to the redrafting of project agreements and rescheduling of project debt, a restructuring of a major international project financing almost inevitably involves the need to work closely with the host government and non-governmental organizations. In many cases, it is government action (e.g. repudiation of a purchase agreement by a government offtaker or changes in taxes or other laws) that created the need for the renegotiation. In other

cases, public and consumer concerns over the level of tariffs for infrastructure projects or over environmental and social aspects of a project may be the cause of restructuring. Because the government and the various non-governmental organizations are often part of the reason why the project experiences problems, they must also be part of the solution and their needs satisfied in the restructuring process if the restructured project is to be sustainable.

7. Potential Problem Areas. There are a number of problems that are often encountered in restructuring international projects. Some are unique to project finance restructurings while others are common to other types of restructuring as well. They include:

- bondholder tranches which present a difficulty when it comes to canvassing the vast number of holders and to voting on proposed changes;

- multilateral development banks who often assert preferred creditor status and refuse to participate in debt rescheduling;

- lack of interim finance for project finance restructuring as there is generally no source of new finance except for existing lenders and project participants; and

- need for 100% approval for changes in some specified terms and conditions. This means that the restructuring process can be prevented by a single holdout creditor who refuses to agree modifications accepted by the others.

C. Lessons From Major Restructurings

The benefits of trying to work out problems that arise in project financings through negotiation rather than arbitration or litigation are illustrated by comparing the experiences of two major power projects in Asia—the Pation Project in Indonesia and the Dabol Project in India. Both projects had high quality sponsors, contractors, lawyers and other advisors who created the basic structure and legal documentation that was typical for major international project financings at the time. Yet, both projects experienced major problems that necessitated renegotiation and restructuring.

Both projects were private power projects designed to provide badly needed electricity to be purchased by government owned distribution companies who were responsible for delivery and sale to the ultimate consumers in Indonesia and India, respectively. The Paiton Project was a 1,230MW coal fired independent power project, and the sponsors were Edison Mission Electric (a US utility), Mitsui & Co Ltd. (a Japanese company serving as contractor) and General Electric Capital Corp (an affiliate of the supplier of some of the power equipment). The financing package included: (1) loans, political risk insurance and guarantees from Japanese and US government agencies (2) a syndicate of commercial banks providing construction period funding with ECA backing; and (3) an international public bond issue. As a result of the Asian financial crisis in the late 1990's, economic activity and the demand for power decreased in Indonesia and the local currency depreciated dramatically against the dollar. These factors resulted in a refusal by the Indonesian government offtaker to take or pay for power from the facility which, in turn, created a crisis which led to the need to renegotiate and restructure.

The Dabhol Project was a 740MW power plant undertaken pursuant to an Indian government program to attract private developers to assist in the expansion of the Indian power supply sector. Enron, the main sponsor of the project, obtained a no-bid contract to carry out the project and subsequently enlisted General Electric and Bechtel (the contractor) as co-sponsors and providers of equity. The debt was provided by a group of lenders that included Indian government owned banks, a syndicate of foreign commercial bank lenders, export credit agencies and the US Overseas Private Investment Corporation (OPIC). OPIC also provided political risk insurance for the sponsors' equity investment and for one of the commercial banks. The World Bank was approached for possible funding but declined to support the project after undertaking an analysis that concluded that the project was not economically viable. After an initial year of operation, demand began to drop and the plant was shut down in 2001 and employees terminated.

In the the Paiton Project, the parties, after an initial period of confrontation and attempts at arbitration and litigation, realized that cooperation would be best for all parties and entered into a standstill agreement while the project was renegotiated and restructured. What had started as a private sector project remained a private project after a successful restructuring. On the other hand, in the Dabhol Project the parties did not make a major effort to cooperate to resolve the problems that arose. There was no standstill arrangement and all parties resorted to a protracted pattern of litigation and arbitration in an effort to maximize their individual interests to the detriment of the overall project. There were over 30 lawsuits, arbitrations and other proceedings involving the various parties associated with the project. What had started as a private sector project ended up with 100% host government control after being taken over and restarted by entities controlled by the government.

CHAPTER 21

DISPUTE SETTLEMENT

In recent years, there has been a major increase in the number of disputes concerning international project financings with the result that project finance dispute settlement has been a growth industry for lawyers. The purpose of this chapter is to provide an overview of the dispute settlement process in the international project finance field.

A. Unique Nature of International Project Finance Dispute Settlement

The numerous, interlinked contracts among parties from different countries create unique dispute resolution problems for an international project financing. These problems include:

- each project agreement could conceivably have its own dispute settlement clause with a different governing law and a different forum for hearing the dispute;

- the possibility that more than one Bilateral Investment Treaty will be applicable to the same project; and

- a project financing is a single transaction involving many interlinked agreements which means that the way disputes are handled in one contract may impact the operation of other contracts and the project as a whole.

These potential problems create the need for very careful planning for dispute resolution at the time that the project is being structured and project documents are being drafted. Lawyers with special expertise in international investment dispute settlement must be consulted as the concession and key project agreements are being negotiated to ensure the use of the most appropriate dispute settlement mechanisms and to minimize the possibility of conflict among the relevant provisions of the various documents.

B. Current Environment

1. Overview. Every international project finance transaction takes place within the context of treaties relating to international investment, national rules and regulations governing investment, and the various project and financial documents governing the internal aspects of the transaction. When faced with a dispute in a project financing, the parties must consult the terms of the relevant treaties, regulations or agreements to see whether any of them will govern the dispute in the specific case and whether they impose any constraints on their freedom of action in making decisions relating to dispute settlement.

2. Bilateral Investment Treaties. (BIT's). In the past two decades there has been a great increase in the number of state-to-state bilateral investment

treaties and other international investment agreements. There are now over 2,500 bilateral investment agreements in addition to numerous preferential trade and investment agreements, regional agreements and multilateral conventions and instruments with provisions relating to international investment such as NAFTA and the Energy Charter.

The basic purpose of a BIT is to promote investment flows between the two countries that are parties to the treaty. To accomplish this objective, most BIT's will contain, *inter alia*, clauses: (1) defining the investors and specific types of investment that are eligible for protection under the BIT; (2) setting forth substantive standards of protection and treatment of an eligible investment and (3) outlining methods available for the settlement of disputes that arise under the treaty. The most common substantive standards found in BIT's include: fair and equitable treatment; national treatment; most favored nation treatment; full protection and security; no expropriation without appropriate compensation; and freedom from denial of justice. The most common form of dispute settlement is arbitration which allows a private sector investor to bring a claim directly against a state alleged to have violated the treaty. Arbitration before the World Bank's International Center for the Settlement of Investment Disputes (ICSID) is commonly specified, but many treaties also allow other methods and venues for dispute resolution.

C. Basic Dispute Settlement Options

There are several options for resolution of disputes in international project financings which range from amicable settlement among the parties to litigation. These options are summarized as follows.

1. Negotiation. Many BIT's and most project documents contain an obligation for the parties to try to negotiate a resolution of differences as a prerequisite to other more binding forms of dispute resolution.

2. Mediation. Mediation is a variant of negotiation sometimes used when the parties are not able to negotiate the resolution of a dispute themselves. It involves the use of an impartial third party to facilitate discussion and, hopefully, agreement among the parties which will enable the parties achieve a new working relationship.

3. Dispute review board. A dispute review board is a mechanism commonly used in connection with EPC contracts to resolve disputes that arise during the construction phase of a project. It is a body that exists during the construction process to hear initially all disputes under a construction contract. If the parties are unable to reach an amicable settlement, all disputes first go to the dispute review board for resolution. If the parties agree with the board's determination, it becomes final and binding. If one party disagrees, a further attempt is made at amicable settlement and then the dispute goes to arbitration if the parties are not able to agree.

4. <u>Arbitration</u>. Arbitration is a dispute resolution method that depends on the consent of both of the parties who also determine the details of the conduct of the arbitration. In any international arbitration, decisions need to be made by the parties on such matters as appointment of arbitrators, rules of procedure, the situs and the governing law. There are two alternative methods of making these decisions: *ad hoc* arbitration and institutional arbitration. In an *ad hoc* arbitration, the parties and their lawyers assume the entire responsibility for establishing the rules of procedure and arranging for the site and conduct of the arbitration. They may choose to use the UNCITRAL rules for ad hoc arbitration which provides an established set of procedures for conducting the process, but the parties remain responsible for organizing the forum and providing all of the necessary support staff and facilities. In institutional arbitration, the parties turn these responsibilities over to a specialized arbitral institution whose purpose is to provide a forum, a set of rules for selecting arbitrators and conducting the arbitration, and administrative support and assistance. Each institution has its own set of rules and procedures and administers and facilitates the arbitral process for a fee.

There are two treaties that facilitate the enforcement of arbitral awards. The New York Convention on Recognition and Enforcement of Arbitral Awards makes it easier to enforce an arbitral award in any of the member countries as it does not permit review on the merits and limits the grounds for challenge The Washington Convention governs the enforcement of final ICSID awards and requires that countries that are ICSID members enforce an ICSID award as if it were a final judgment of its highest domestic court.

5.   Litigation: Host country court systems often have characteristics that make participants hesitate before using litigation to resolve disputes arising out of major project financings. Many foreign investors are reluctant to use the courts and judges of the host country to resolve disputes because of fear of local bias or concern that local court judges may lack the specialized technical expertise sometimes needed in complex project financings. While arbitration permits the parties to determine the rules of procedure, the use of litigation means national rules of court procedure must be used which may limit flexibility and party options. The awards of national courts are subject to appeal domestically and are often difficult to enforce in other countries as it may depend on treaties providing for reciprocal enforcement of judgments. The combination of these factors has meant that most recent disputes arising out of international project finance transactions have been resolved by international investment arbitration rather than litigation.

D.   Relevant International Investment Arbitration Issues

1.   Umbrella clause. An umbrella clause in a BIT enables a breach of a project related contractual obligation by one of the BIT parties to be used as the basis for a claim under a BIT. A typical umbrella clause would read:

"Each Contracting Party shall observe any
other obligation it has entered into with
regard to investments in its territory
by investors of the other
Contracting Party"

This language means that if a government breaches
an obligation in one of the project agreements, it
could be subject to the dispute settlement provisions of the BIT because it violated the umbrella
clause which says that it must honor all obligations
with foreign investors. This result would be possible
even though the dispute resolution clause in the
contract that was violated called for another forum
for dispute settlement and even though the contract
breach is relatively minor and does not indepen-
dently violate any of the government's substantive
obligations for treatment of investors contained in
the BIT.

2.   Anti-arbitration injunction. In several projects where the foreign investor has attempted to
use arbitration to resolve disputes, the local courts
have restricted resort to arbitration by intervening
through the use of an anti-arbitration injunction. A
host country court might issue an injunction to
delay or block arbitration in order to enable the
government or another local party to seek judicial
review of its claim that the project contracts are
invalid or unenforceable. For example, both the
Paiton Project in Indonesia and the Dabhol Project
in India discussed in the previous chapter involved
anti-arbitration injunctions when the foreign investor attempted to use arbitration to resolve disputes.

3. Challenges to the Jurisdiction of the Arbitral Tribunal. In many international investment arbitrations brought under the dispute settlement provisions of a BIT, there is a challenge to jurisdiction of the arbitral tribunal. There are a variety of grounds for this challenge, including: there is no "investment" within the meaning of the BIT; the investor bringing the claim does not have the benefit of the treaty because it is not a resident or citizen of one of the contracting states; and the investment violated the laws of the host government with respect to entry. Many claims under BIT's are rejected by tribunals on jurisdictional grounds with the result that there is never a hearing on the alleged violations of the substantive provisions designed to provide protection to investors. This means that lawyers for investors must plan carefully to ensure that the investment meets all of the jurisdictional requirements of the relevant BIT.

Appendix 1

EXAMPLE OF A GENERIC PROJECT RISK MATRIX

Risk Category	Type of Project Risk	Type of Risk Protection For Lenders
Resource	Size and nature of reserves. Continued availability of the reserve	Independent evaluation by more than one geological consulting firm. Dedication of the reserves to the project. Supply or pay contract. Producer agrees to make up any shortfall from another source.
Market	Inaccurate demand estimates. Overcapacity emerges. New technology lowers the price of the product from other sources. The price at which the output can be sold becomes uneconomic.	More than one independent market surveys. Various types of contractual arrangements, including long term purchase contract at fixed minimum payment or a deficiency agreement. Use of derivatives to hedge commodity price risk.
Country and Political Risk	Economic or political instability in the host country. Relationship between host and home countries deteriorates. Home country restrictions on foreign investment Expropriation.	Political risk insurance. Multilateral consortia of sponsors and lenders. MDB or ECA involvement to create "halo effect". Advance exchange control approval.

206

Risk Category	Type of Project Risk	Type of Risk Protection For Lenders
	Exchange controls. New laws or regulations introduced after project starts impact project operation and cost. Government approvals not received in satisfactory form or arbitrarily withdrawn.	Trust arrangements which segregate the revenue stream outside of the host country. Host country has a stake in the success of the project. Joint venture with local sponsors. Use of stabilization clause in project documentation.
Financial	Interest rate on borrowings is floating and rates increase. Debt service obligation is in one currency and revenues in another currency. SPV defaults on debt obligations. Refinancing risk.	Use of derivatives to mitigate interest rate and currency risks. Matching currency of revenue with currency of debt service. Credit guarantee Long maturity loans.
Technical	Unexpected technical problems in construction or operation. New technology is used and has start up problems. Technology becomes obsolete.	Independent analysis of technology being used. Use of high quality engineers and contractors. Guaranty or warranty of technology by supplier or operator. Commercial insurance
Environmental, Social and Community Reaction	Environmental or community opposition delays construction or forces shutdown or alteration in project. New environmental or safety requirements cause large cost increases.	Sensitivity to environmental, social and human rights issues in project planning and preparation. Consultation with environmental and community groups. Use of competent, qualified experts. Stabilization clause.
Legal	Difficulty of negotiating contracts between parties with different	Obtain high quality legal advice, including local counsel.

Risk Category	Type of Project Risk	Type of Risk Protection For Lenders
	legal systems. Inability to obtain adequate security interest in project assets. Inadequate local courts and legal system. Weak regulatory system	Create workable alternative dispute settlement mechanisms.
Force Majeure	Unanticipated event (e.g. natural disaster or action of host government) prevents a party from performing and excuses performance.	Adequate commercial and political risk insurance. Careful coordination of force majeure clauses in project documents.
Construction Phase	Cost overruns due, <u>inter alia</u>, to risk factors noted above create funding problems and/or make project uneconomic. One or more of above risk factors result in non-completion and abandonment of the project. Project completed but does not meet performance expectations.	<u>Cost Overruns.</u> Fixed price, turnkey contract. Independent expert check on cost estimates and technology. Adequate contingencies built into finance plan. Overrun funding commitment by sponsors or other form of standby funding arrangement. <u>Completion of Project</u> Drawdown equity first to protect lenders. Performance bonds from contractor. Equipment supplier warranties. Tough "completion tests" Completion agreement (i.e. fund completion or repay outstanding debt)
Operational Phase	Interruption or diminution of the revenue stream from one or more of above risks.	Contractual arrangements to assure minimum revenue adequate to service debt.

Risk Category	Type of Project Risk	Type of Risk Protection For Lenders
		Insurance. Guarantees of debt and/or specific risks.

Appendix 2

DUE DILIGENCE CHECKLIST

1. <u>Host Country.</u> The purpose of the due diligence with respect to the host country is to assess the general climate for investment in the country in which the project will be carried out. The analysis covers such areas as:

- macroeconomic situation

- political stability

- tax and foreign investment laws and the consistency of their application

- dispute resolution process and the independence of the judiciary

- foreign exchange regime and a forecast of future foreign exchange rates

- good governance and corruption issues

2. <u>Project Participants.</u> The purpose of this analysis is to evaluate who will carry out the project and the creditworthiness, financial strength and commitment of each key participant in the project. It would include analysis of:

- the project sponsors, including creditworthiness and experience in similar projects

- other project participants (contractors; suppliers of equipment and other essential inputs; users or off-takers; operators; lenders; key advisers; and other parties essential for the success of the project)

- the nature and strength of each participant's financial situation, experience in similar projects and commitment to the project

- the host government's commitment to the project and its willingness to provide cooperation and support

- the quality of the advisors and consultants to the project

3. Basic Organization and Structure. The evaluation of this topic considers the nature of the borrowing entity and how the project is to be organized and structured during both the construction and operational phases of the project. It would assess:

- the sponsor and other ownership interests in the project

- the terms of any shareholder agreements dealing with amount and nature of contributions, management, restrictions on sale and other intra-sponsor matters

- the nature of the proposed borrowing entity

- the nature of the entity that will carry out the project (if different than the borrowing entity)

- the legal and tax factors that influence the proposed organization and structure of the project

4. <u>Basic Economic Viability of the Project.</u> The economic viability assessment looks at the market in which the project will be operating in order to determine the prospects for the viability of the project. The assessment would include:

- market studies of current and future demand for the project's product or service
- analysis of the level, certainty and predictability of revenue flows over the life of the project
- competitive factors
- other factors which could affect the future viability of the project

5. <u>Quality of Project Preparation.</u> The purpose of this analysis is to evaluate how well the project has been prepared. It includes analysis of:

- the quality of the feasibility and design studies
- the quality of geological studies for mining and petroleum projects
- the quality of hydrological studies for hydro and other water projects
- the quality of the cost estimates for the project
- procurement procedures
- any environmental analysis that has been done
- acquisition of needed land or rights of way and site clearance

- the tax planning for the project
- the preliminary financial and legal assessments
- accounting systems to be used in connection with the project

6. <u>Project Risk and Insurance/Hedging Analysis.</u> The purpose of this analysis is to ensure that all material project risks have been identified and avoided, mitigated or transferred to the maximum extent possible within the context of available risk management techniques, including insurance and hedging. The main areas of risk that are analyzed include:

- overall risk assessment
- technical risks
- human resource risks
- natural resource risks
- market risks, including the risk of competition
- construction risks, including both completion and overrun risks
- risks of interruption of the stream(s) of revenue generated by the project
- general financial risks
- foreign exchange risks
- credit risks
- interest rate risks
- insurance and hedging possibilities

7.   Technical and Design. The purpose of the technical due diligence is to ensure that the technology and design are feasible and appropriate for the project. It would include assessment of:

- the nature of the technology and design
- whether the technology and design are new and novel or whether they are tested and proven
- the quality of the engineering and design consultants
- the adequacy and state of preparation of the project site

8.   Procurement. The procurement process is reviewed to assess whether the most appropriate method of procurement was used and whether all relevant laws and regulations were followed. Factors considered include:

- the applicable procurement laws and regulations
- the nature of the procurement process used (e.g. competitive bidding; unsolicited bid; sole source contract)
- how the various elements of the project were bundled for procurement purposes
- the clarity and quality of the bidding documents
- the openness and transparency of the procurement process
- assurances of equality of opportunity and treatment for all bidders

- the nature and competence of the bid evaluation panel
- the nature and extent of any post award negotiations on the terms of the concession or other contract
- whether there were any protests by losing bidders and how these protests were resolved.

9.   Construction Plan. The purpose of the due diligence in this area is to assess the feasibility of the construction time schedule and estimated completion date which is critical for the commencement of revenue flows from the project. It would include assessment of:

- quality of contractors and their experience in similar projects
- reliability of the construction cost estimates
- reliability of the estimated completion date
- adequacy of contingency or overrun funding
- construction of needed ancillary and support facilities (e.g. roads)
- whether a turnkey contract was involved.

10.   Operational Matters. The due diligence on the proposed operation of the project is intended to asses the experience and quality of the proposed operator and identify potential operational phase problems. It would analyze:

- the nature and availability of key operational inputs (e.g. coal, gas or oil for thermal power projects)

- the quality and experience of the proposed operator

- the terms and conditions of any Operation and Maintenance Agreement

- typical operational problems that have arisen in similar projects

11.   Financial Model and Projections. The analysis of the financial model and financial projections made for a project assesses their quality and realism in light of the economic prospects for the project. It would include:

- review of the assumptions used in creating the financial model, construction and operating budgets, the revenue flows, borrowing costs, debt amortization and other key variables used in running the financial projections

- profitability, rate of return and debt coverage

- sensitivity analysis

- the experience and quality of the preparer of the financial model

12.   Finance Plan. The analysis of the finance plan ensures that the most appropriate sources of finance have been identified and that there are no gaps in the finance plan. Such analysis covers:

- the rating of debt (if applicable)

- market capacity studies

- evaluation of the basic alternative sources of finance

- the basic terms and conditions of the proposed financing.

- assessment of the possibility of refinancing risk

13.   General Legal and Regulatory Considerations. This part of the due diligence determines the legal feasibility of the project and ensures that all legal and regulatory risks and issues have been identified. Factors considered include:

- the preliminary legal feasibility analysis

- the regulatory regime for the project

- dispute settlement options, including arbitration, governing law and forum for dispute resolution

14.   Key Contract Documents, including Concessions. This topic is especially important for long term lenders and is designed to ensure that loans are protected and secured by appropriate and legally binding documentation. Analysis would include:

- the terms and conditions of the key contracts and credit support arrangements for the project including concession agreements (and other licenses necessary to carry out the project), offtake and supply contracts, essential leases, construction contracts, operating and maintenance agreements, financing documents, guarantees, insurance, shareholder agreements and other key documents

- security over project assets, contracts and the revenue stream

- whether the key contracts have been duly approved and authorized and the persons signing the contracts have proper signing authority

15.   Environmental Considerations. This aspect of due diligence is to be sure that any environmental factors (including relocation of people and archeological considerations) are identified and dealt with. Factors reviewed include:

- need for an environmental assessment
- any environmental assessment that has been produced
- compliance with local environmental law
- need for relocation of people.

16.   Consultation with Affected Communities and Human Rights Issues. Every major international project will impact the local community and affect the lives of those affected by the project's construction and operation. Due diligence in this area would review:

- the adequacy of sponsor consultation with affected communities to insure that local input was obtained
- potential human rights issues
- likelihood of claims based on failure to consult or alleged human rights abuses (e.g. action under the Alien Tort Claims Act)

Appendix 3

ANNOTATED CHECKLIST OF PROVISIONS INCLUDED IN CONCESSIONS

There is no standard form of concession as the terms of each agreement are determined by a combination of factors peculiar to the country, sector and project under consideration. There are, however, several matters that are commonly dealt with in concession agreements, and they are listed in this annotated checklist.

Scope and Nature of the Agreement

- formal grant
- objective and purpose
- extent and coverage
- duration, possibility of extension and ultimate expiration
- requirements for re-bidding
- assignability and transfer

Parties to the Agreement

- The sovereign state itself should be a party to the contract and the sole government party should not be a government agency or a sub-sovereign governmental entity.

- It is common for there to be more than one governmental party to the agreement—e.g. the sovereign state and a government agency responsible for the relevant sector.
- In the case of agreements with state or municipal governments, the issue is more complicated and depends on the country's constitution and laws dealing with the division of power and the basic structure of government.

Exclusivity of Concession Rights

- nature and scope of the right to undertake the project
- Concessionaires and lenders prefer exclusive rights
- Governments often agree not to grant competing concession rights or engage in competing activities through government controlled entities.

Scope and Nature of the Project

- project description
- geographic coverage
- design specifications and facility requirements
- performance output and quality standards and requirements

Nature of the Private Participant

- ownership and shareholding, including minimum equity requirements

- restrictions on transfer of share ownership
- nationality and/or local ownership requirements
- local content and local sub-contracting requirements
- personnel: local hiring and limits on foreign workers
- composition and citizenship requirements of board of directors

Basic Obligations of the Private Participant

- meet construction standards and schedule
- operate the facility in accordance with performance specifications/standards
- make all payments of concession fees to the government
- select and oversee contractor
- meet any ongoing investment, expansion and maintenance obligations
- meet all obligations associated with the transfer of assets back to the government at the end of the concession

Basic Obligations of the Government

- make site available for construction after proper site clearance and creation of access
- make ancillary services available such as temporary power and water

- facilitate construction and operation of the project through assistance in the approval process, obtaining necessary legislative and political clearance
- monitor and inspect project on a timely basis

Government Support Obligations

- specification of conditions precedent to the grant of support
- fiscal incentives or exemptions
- customs duty exemptions
- special treatment under local labor laws for work permits, expatriate taxation and remittance of salary
- obligation to facilitate implementation and operation of the project and refrain from interference to the economic and financial detriment of the project
- performance guarantees of government owned entities
- price subsidies to poorer consumers or other politically sensitive groups
- fuel subsidies
- direct credit and other financial guarantees

Payments to the Government

- The host government can receive revenue from a project carried out under a concession in a number of ways, including taxation, an initial lump sum payment, a fixed canon or concession fee payable on a periodic basis, a share of revenue or profits or through dividends as a shareholder.

- concession fees and/or profit sharing and the method of calculation
- provisions for the adjustment of the government's share
- taxes

Design and Engineering

- approval of design and engineering plans and construction schedule
- process for agreeing any deviations in the plans and schedule

Construction

- specification of construction standards and schedule
- site clearance and availability issues
- possible requirement as to nature of the construction contract (e.g. fixed price turnkey contract)
- possible preference to local subcontractors
- meet performance standards
- supervision, monitoring and inspection, including possible requirement to use an independent engineer or a quality assurance inspector
- bonding, insurance and other risk mitigation

- completion tests
- contractor penalties/bonuses for late/early completion

Operation

- specification of performance tests and operational standards that must be met
- maintenance obligations
- any ongoing investment or expansion obligations
- ongoing insurance obligations
- provision for temporary takeover by the government in an emergency situation
- ongoing role of the relevant regulatory body

Pricing of the Project's Output or Service

- role of the regulatory body in price determination and adjustment
- pricing methodology or formula
- price adjustment provisions over the life of the concession (i.e. automatic adjustment through various indexing formulae, by the regulatory process on a periodic basis or one time discretionary adjustment due to unforeseen change in circumstances)
- cross subsidy among classes of consumers
- government subsidy of price paid to certain classes of consumers

Accounting, Audit and Project Management

- specification of accounting and audit standards
- obligation of concessionaire to devote adequate resources to ongoing project management in terms of quantity and quality of personnel, equipment and funding

Lender Provisions

- Since the concession or other basic project document is the key operational document, it is carefully reviewed by potential lenders to ensure that it will be bankable—i.e. that it contains adequate safeguards as to completion, reliability of the revenue stream, enforcement of security and payments in event of early termination to serve as the basis for lending to the project.
- If lenders feel that the contract is not adequate, they will require, as a pre-condition for agreeing to a loan, the inclusion of clauses to make the agreement "bankable." The most common of these clauses are:
  - adequacy of revenue stream
  - adequacy of security, including security in the concession itself
  - step-in-rights
  - ability of the concessionaire to assign its rights under the concession to the lender
  - repayment of outstanding loans in event of termination

- dispute settlement provisions
- Lenders may insist on clause requiring government to enter into a Direct Agreement with the lenders.

Early Termination

- events of default that give rise to a right of early termination by either the government or the private participant
- rights to cure any event of default to prevent termination
- step-in-rights for lenders enabling them to assume the rights of the concessionaire
- procedures to be followed in the event of default, including cooperation between the government and the lenders to find an alternative private sector partner
- compensation in the event of termination, including the possibility of liquidated damages and the lenders' need to have assurances that there will be adequate funds to pay any debt outstanding at termination
- lender ability to take security in the concession itself in the event of termination and the ability to assign the contract to a new private sector partner.
- Specific defaults that give rise to termination will vary from project to project by may include:

- default by the concessionaire on the loans to the project;

- failure of the concessionaire to meet the specified performance or investment obligations in a timely manner;

- bankruptcy, dissolution or liquidation of the concessionaire

- failure by the government to make the site available, provide the necessary rights-of-way or honor the tariff provisions of the concession with respect to rates or rate adjustment; and

- failure by the government to compensate the concessionaire in the event of a "materially adverse state action."

- In addition to actions by the parties, a right to terminate may arise as a result of events outside the control of either party such as a force majeure event or a change in circumstances that leads to economic hardship or destroys the economic balance or equilibrium of the transaction.

- In some countries the government has a unilateral right to terminate even if no party is at fault, and some countries may limit the concessionaire's right to terminate certain types of concessions even if the government is in default.

Normal Termination Date and Transfer Back Provisions

- options available on scheduled termination date of the concession, including extension of the concession, rebidding, or transfer of project assets back to the government
- specification of concessionaire's obligations upon normal termination, including return of assets in satisfactory working condition.

Security Interests

- description of the nature of security interests in both tangible and intangible project assets, including the concession itself
- the government's obligation to cooperate in registering and enforcing lender security in project assets
- assignability of security interests
- ability to acquire a security interest in the contract rights

Force Majeure and other Relief Events

- Concessions often contain extended provisions defining what constitutes *force majeure,* hardship, material adverse state action and other relief events and specify actions to be taken if such event occurs.

Waiver of Sovereign Immunity

- Concessionaires and lenders will seek an explicit waiver of sovereign immunity stating that activities under the concession are commercial in nature so that the host government can be sued and its assets attached in the event that it defaults on its obligations under the concession.

Dispute Settlement

- form or method of dispute settlement ranging from informal resolution by the parties themselves, mediation, arbitration to formal court proceedings
- determination of the place of the settlement proceedings: host country; home country or neutral location
- the choice of governing law: host country law; home country law; third country law (generally England or New York); general principles of international law
- role of applicable bilateral investment treaties.

Changes in the Agreement

- Concessions may contain provisions dealing with the circumstances in which the terms and conditions of the contract may be altered to meet changing circumstances that will be inevitable over the life of the agreement.
- In many countries with a civil law tradition, the host government retains a unilateral right to alter the contract for public policy reasons; and, for obvious reasons, the private participants and their lenders seek to limit this right to the maximum extent possible.
- In other countries amendments may be made to restore the original economic balance or

equilibrium after mutual agreement when there are circumstances that materially affect the private partner's economic return.

Separability

- A separability clause provides that, if one or more clauses of an agreement are declared invalid (or become non-operative for other reasons), this does not make the entire contract invalid and that the parties will, if necessary, endeavor to negotiate new provisions to deal with the void.

Role of Regulatory Agencies

- identification of the agency (or agencies) with jurisdiction

- nature and extent of jurisdiction

Various Annexes

- Concession often have extensive annexes which contain details of a number of the matters noted above. They would typically cover:
  - technical specifications
  - completion tests (physical, technical and financial completion)
  - calculation of liquidated damages
  - pricing methodology and adjustment
  - technical provisions relating to the condition of project assets when returned to the government at the expiration of the concession

Appendix 4

OUTLINE OF PROVISIONS A COMMON TERMS AGREEMENT

Among

SPV BORROWER

THE VARIOUS LENDERS

VARIOUS FACILITY AGENTS

VARIOUS TRUSTEES

THE COLLATERAL AGENT

THE INTERCREDITOR AGENT

TABLE OF CONTENTS

INDEX

A

DERIVATIVES
As due diligence issue, 35
Basic forms, 171–172
Documentation, 173–174
General nature and uses, 171–173
Intercreditor issues, 176–178
Limitations and risks, 175–176
Loan agreement clauses, 175
Used in project finance, 174–175

DESIGN DEFECTS, 86

DIAGRAMS
Concept of project finance, 7
Debt financing documentation, 146
Operational waterfall account, 170

DISADVANTAGES OF PROJECT FINANCE, 20–21

DIRECT AGREEMENTS, 140–141

DISPUTE SETTLEMENT
Anti-arbitration injunction, 204
Arbitral tribunal jurisdiction, 205
Basic options
    Arbitration, 202–203
    Dispute review board, 201
    Litigation, 203
    Mediation, 201
    Negotiation, 201
Bilateral investment treaties, 35, 199–200, 203, 205
Enforcement of arbitral awards, 202–203
Governing law, 55, 71, 78, 202, 217
In concessions, 78
Need to coordinate clauses, 71
Review of arbitral awards, 202
Umbrella clause, 203
Unique nature in project finance, 198

DUE DILIGENCE
Checklist, 210–218
Derivatives, 35
General, 29
Environment, human rights and community relations, 34
International investment law, 35
Legal due diligence, 31–33
Public private partnerships, 34
Security in project assets, 138–140

†